THE WARRIOR WAY

LIVING COUNTER TO THE CULTURE

Sean Dunn

TATE PUBLISHING, LLC

Published in the United States of America
by Tate Publishing, LLC
127 East Trade Center Terrace
Mustang, OK 73064
(888) 361–9473

ISBN: 1–5988638–2-7

DEDICATION

This book is dedicated to all who know their faith is supposed to affect their lives; and their lives were meant to impact their generation.

May you model authentic faith and attractive Christianity. May the world recognize that you live by a different code and for a greater cause.

I pray that your inner warrior be unleashed, as you pursue Christ with an aggressive faith.

The Warrior Way

Living Counter to the Culture

INTRODUCTION

Sometimes when I read the Bible, I forget that the men and women that I am reading about were just like me. They had fears, anxieties, emotions, and failure littering their past.

Often, I picture these people as superhuman: God speaks to them, and without any thought of the consequence, the inconvenience, or the improbability of the task, they run off in faith to achieve the goal. Because the Bible paints many characters as stick figures, failing to describe much of their humanity and frailties, it makes them unrelateable and sets them up as an unattainable standard.

In my faith journey, this standard has brought confusion, frustration, and self-doubt. As I have searched for answers to my questions and energy to pursue an aggressive faith, I have looked not for a quote that inspires, but lives of greatness that I can learn from and lean on. Interested in finding keys that will bring me stability, strength, endurance, and victories, I have chosen to study warriors of the past—biblical heroes as well as contemporary giants of faith and ministry.

Trying to discover personal faith and overcome fear, I have looked beyond their actions to uncover the attitudes, perspectives, and motives that have either led them to victory (so that I can imitate them) or initiated their demise (so I am aware of what to avoid). This book is a result of the education that I am receiving.

Even as I wrote this book, I was confronted with my weaknesses, insecurities, pride, and many other things that need improvement (in the pages ahead, you will join me on this journey); however, in the midst of the issues that I continue to press through, I have discovered God's grace, mercy, forgiveness, and strength that have inspired in me determination, conviction, and hope.

I still have a long way to go, but I am learning and growing in the ways of my Lord and my heroes. I am being challenged and instructed daily. This journey is teaching me to reject normality (defined by casual Christianity) in order to pursue the life of surrender and service—the life of a soldier.

By God's grace, I am learning to live *The Warrior Way.*

CHAPTER 1

Calling: The Journey Begins

Isaiah's defining moment—the one that changed the course of his life—is recorded in Isaiah chapter 6.

The prophet was caught up into a place where God's presence was so strong and his revelation so overwhelming that he realized his sin and confessed his guilt. With six-winged angelic beings constantly circling God's throne and declaring his praise with otherworldly volume shaking the threshold of the temple, Isaiah volunteered for service.

Just like Isaiah, in one solemn, although unplanned, assembly with God, the cry of my heart was amplified, the instabilities were exposed and addressed, and I realized that my desire to live as a warrior was not my idea, but his.

Growing up in the '80s, I was a typical boy: I liked sports, chased girls, and attracted trouble. My life was consistently inconsistent and routinely random. There were times when I was kind and polite, others when I was obnoxious and rude, times when I followed my friends and times when I led.

Few things in my life captivated my attention for long stretches. Although I did well in school, my focus on academics was not sustained after the bell had rung and the homework was done. Music was enjoyed, but I was not a fanatic and certainly not a groupie. Athletics appealed to me, but which sport I chose varied season-to-season and occasionally day-to-day. Even my friends were interchangeable without much thought. If Tony was available, I would hang out with him, but if not, Troy, Jeff, or Jodi could take his place.

This lifestyle of sporadic pursuits and arbitrary interests even affected my faith. Although I had grown up in a Christian home where the principles of the Bible were presented as absolutes, my interest in them and ability to apply them was conditional. My lifestyle was not driven by my faith as much as my faith was driven by my lifestyle. On days when I was in church and around Christian influences, my spiritual convictions were at the forefront. But when life slipped secular, I rarely thought about God, Jesus, church, or the way those things should affect me.

"My lifestyle was not driven by my faith as much as my faith was driven by my lifestyle."

The duplicity of this life went mostly unnoticed to me. Occasionally, a gifted speaker would spark the realization that there was a disconnection between my beliefs and my lifestyle, but after a quick prayer, I would comfortably slip back into a life of spiritual neglect and selfish hunts.

I was not overly immoral or overtly hypocritical, mind you. I was simply living a life of apathy and disregard as it pertained to my faith. When away from church, I routinely ignored the Bible, loved only myself, prayed only for meals, and never acted on spiritual things.

Gazing back at my history, I would have to say that 90% of my thoughts were as shallow as a wading pool. But in the midst of seeking entertainment, pursuing popularity, and striving to squeeze excitement out of my teen years, my heart and mind did beat together in regard to one thing biblical—I wanted to make a difference. I wanted to be a warrior.

I rarely thought about the abundant life that was promised, yet something inside of me wanted to tell others about this incredible gift. Even though I disregarded the majority of the teachings, I knew that the Bible was true, Jesus was the only way to heaven, and everyone—EVERYONE—needed to know.

Every so often, an urgent pounding in my chest reminded me that I was to do more than perform my faith as a play, painting my character to be the hero bathed in esteem and suaveness. I knew I was created to be a living storybook of God's grace, power, and love. I was to be fearless, stable, and effective. I was convinced that my faith was to affect both my life and the world; but that is not how I lived.

Although the casual Christianity that I had embraced contradicted the high calling and strong desires I randomly sensed, the urge to be used by God continued to grow. Vivid pictures of proclaiming truth began to visit my daydreams. Snapshots of mountain-moving faith began to interrupt my selfish life. My social interest in people started to experience conflict with my desire for them to understand spiritual realities.

I don't know how long the clash lasted—maybe months, maybe years. However, its intensity brought frustration and confusion couched in self-doubt. Each time I started to take positive steps acting on my desires to live a faith-filled life, I was quickly ambushed and overpowered by the reality that I was weak, inconsistent, and unreliable.

But at 14 years old, my life of chaos was confronted. I had my Isaiah 6 encounter that forever changed my life.

It happened on a Sunday night. I walked into church unsuspecting, unaware that the service was going to turn personal. Sitting down with my friends, we began to chat. Our conversation became quieter but continued sporadically through worship music and the first part of the speaker's message. But somewhere in that routine experience something changed. I sensed an incredible presence invading my space. It was both beautiful and uncomfortable, exhilarating and terrifying. I could not move. My friends continued to talk but I did not—I could not.

For at least 30 minutes, I sat with labored breath and complete focus, as things around me seemed insignificant. During those 30 minutes, the pastor had ended his talk, all of the people in the auditorium had gone home, and my friends had loudly departed, but I could not bring myself to leave.

As I sat there, body glued to the seat and heart attentive to God, for the first time in my life, I sensed the awesomeness of my Creator. I cannot adequately explain it except to say that I was caught off guard by the beauty of the Lord and undone by his holiness.

I wanted to look away but knew that I would regret it if I did. His holiness revealed my depravity. I had not been ready for this.

I thought I had perfected the art of keeping conviction away, yet here it came—like a tidal wave. I realized that I lacked faith, power, and conviction. I was reminded of sins committed as well as times when I had missed opportunities to share God's goodness because of my own selfish plans. I grunted in disgust, *"Oh, God. Forgive me."*

After several minutes spent in rehearsing and confessing the attitudes, frailties, and insecurities that had led to sin in the past, I sensed forgiveness. Joy entered—but the intensity of this encounter was not yet over.

Out of respect for the awesome presence of God and wanting to repay him for the kindness that he had just shown to me, I picked up my Bible and made a promise. *"God, if you can use me, do it. I will go wherever you lead me, and I will say whatever you tell me to say. My life is yours."*

Without any hesitation, God spoke. A phrase dropped into my heart that I understood to be the gentle whisper of the Holy Spirit. *"Contend for a Generation."*

At the time, I did not know what it meant. I was not sure how it translated into the life of a 14-year-old boy, but I grabbed hold of it as if it were my marching orders. Opening my blue King James Bible and flipping to the back, I wrote down that phrase as I responded in prayer telling God that I would if he would teach me how.

Over 20 years ago, I wrote that phrase for the first time. As I wrote it, God engraved it on my heart.

That was Just the Beginning

I am just one of the thousands that God has apprehended throughout the years. From biblical times until heaven is revealed, God has been and will continue to seek and discover men and women who are willing to enlist their lives to serve as knights and warriors in his army.

"From biblical times until heaven is revealed, God has been and will continue to seek and discover men and women who are willing to enlist their lives to serve as knights and warriors in his army."

The eyes of the Lord are continually moving across the earth searching for people he can build into champions of courage and faith. He seeks hearts that are willing to reject normality (defined by casual Christianity) in order to pursue the Creator—fearless men who will speak the truth and stand up for righteousness, faith-filled women who live by conviction and walk in love. These are the people our Leader is looking for. When he discovers such commitment and surrender, he promises to prove himself strong both in and through that life. (II Chronicles 16:9)

Years ago, God found me in a moment of willing submission. That day, he marked me and I have never been the same.

He identified me that day, but he is still shaping my identity. In the pages ahead, I will give you glimpses into the journey of faith I have been on as I have worked (yes, it has been work) to get close to Christ. I have studied to understand my calling, and prayed to surrender my will to him on a daily basis. My learning curve includes trial and error, accomplishments and mistakes along with some lessons learned in the strangest possible ways. But mostly it comes through observation and study.

In seeking to fully grasp the purpose for which I was created, I have invested time in studying role models of warrior exploits and stunning faith. Through investigating the lives of great men and women of faithfulness and action, I have seen glimpses of the courage I long to have, the character I need, and convictions that I believe are from God. These people have inspired in me hope that one day

I, too, can overcome intimidation, destroy insecurity, defeat sin, and be used by God to change the culture.

I invite you along for the ride as I share some of the education I have received. Although this is not intended to be an autobiography, many of these chapters are uncomfortably personal. It would be easier to hide behind a façade that declares, "I have arrived," but that would not be honest nor would it be beneficial. I pray that the discoveries and the mistakes I have made offer you clarity so you will be able to avoid the potholes that could slow you down.

By God's grace, I am learning to live The Warrior Way. Perhaps we can gain understanding together.

Chapter One Summary

The Journey Begins

Thought For The Day:

God created you intentionally and specifically. You have a purpose. If you allow Him to, God will show you what that is.

Scripture Theme:

2 Chronicles 16:9 "For the eyes of the Lord range throughout the earth to strengthen those whose hearts are fully committed to him."

Questions To Ponder:

Have you had a defining moment in your life & if so what did you do with that moment?

Is your lifestyle driving your faith or is your faith driving your lifestyle?

Digging Deeper:

To read more about Isaiah's encounter read: Isaiah 6:1-10.

CHAPTER 2

Preparation:
Before The Battle Begins

Ok, let's start…at the beginning.

Just because the will to war has been discovered and the calling embraced, does not mean victory is ensured. Many would-be warriors do not live successful and stable lives because they avoid the preparation that moves them from hopeful to capable, from people with potential to ones fulfilling promise.

The ones who will overcome sin, shed light into dark areas, and shape their generation are the ones that understand that God will shape them in private as he prepares them to be used in public. This is the process that builds the warrior, sculpts his faith, and molds his life.

This is the method that God used to shape Samuel into the man who (although he is not recorded as fighting in any skirmishes) spoke prophetically to God's people. He lived his life in boldness no matter the circumstances. This is why I list him among the warriors who inspire me.

Samuel was not always bold—as a matter of fact, the Bible records a time when he was confused and meek. A gift from God to a barren mother, he was dedicated back to the Lord as a young child. He was set apart for service before the Lord.

When God glanced at the child Samuel, he knew why he created him—to anoint kings, train prophets, listen to and speak for the Lord, and train the people of God—but he saw one who was not ready to fulfill his full purpose. His heart was pure and his faith growing, but he was raw. Unfortunately, Samuel did not have the best spiritual mentors. Eli, the priest, was old and had become lazy. He was ignoring sin, allowing practices that were dishonoring to the priesthood to continue, and failing to confront the main culprits that were destroying the credibility of the post—his sons. Perhaps he was tired…perhaps he was afraid. Perhaps his old age had him thinking about retirement instead of responsibility. We do not know why he remained silent, but we do know that God was not pleased.

Eli was about to be replaced.

God wanted to speak, but he had not found anyone who would listen. He needed a priest who would pay attention and obey, one who would pursue his heart and learn what was on his mind (I Samuel 2:35). That is why God came recruiting a prophet/warrior.

"God wanted to speak, but he had not found anyone who would listen."

History has recorded that Samuel *"grew up in the presence of God"* (I Samuel 2:21). That means that he lived openly before the Almighty. He went out of his way to be near him. You get a glimpse of his heart when you learn that he would lie down in the temple of the Lord, where the ark of God was (I Samuel 3:1–3).

Although a typical boy with desires to kick up his heels and let down his hair, he did not neglect God's presence. God had not yet spoken to him, yet his growing faith is what determined what he did and where he went with his spare time. Because Samuel positioned himself in God's presence, God was able to prepare him to influence history. It worked for him. It proved to be the key step in my spiritual maturity as well.

Branded by my calling and submitted to it, I walked out of the church that night with my marching orders, but a long way to go. I was willing—but was I able? The answer to that question was, "Not yet." My willing spirit had proven that it could easily be overpowered by my weak flesh. My laziness, self-ishness, pride, duplicity, and rebellion against God's intentions for me were going to hold me back until something changed inside of me.

"My willing spirit had proven that it could easily be overpowered by my weak flesh."

That transformation began to take place a couple of months later, as I took a dare from my youth pastor to begin investing time in my spiritual life every day. Truthfully, I accepted his challenge to prove to him that nothing in my life would change if I did something as monotonous and meaningless as read a historic book and pray internal prayers inviting God to speak to me. Thankfully, I was proven wrong.

My attitude about the Bible and prayer was not healthy at the time that I took the dare. Because I had been told my entire life that I needed to do devotions, I had found that obligation burdensome and not rewarding. I had made commitments to sustain those practices before, but I had lost interest after a time, as the task proved boring. I questioned the modern day validity of a book that was written and compiled in centuries long past.

It is not that I doubted the inspiration of the Bible. I have always believed that God instigated every word. My problem came in both the practice of finding time to read it daily and believing that it spoke to the condition of my generation and my times.

As I undertook the task of testing my theory, I was caught off guard by both the impact that it immediately had on my life and the inspiration that I began to receive from it.

At that point in my life, my self-perception was dominated with my failures to overcome sins in the areas of stealing, lying, and lustful thoughts. However, after just three months of faithfully investing time in his Word and introspective prayer, those strongholds began to lose their grip.

My youth pastor told me that if I was faithful in my time with God, he would change my heart, but I did not believe him. It turns out, he knew what he was talking about and I was benefiting because of it.

My perception about the book was beginning to change as well. Instead of dreading my obligation,

I began to look forward to reading. What started as a discipline quickly turned into an enjoyable habit as I began to discover joy when uncovering incredible stories of historic significance. The battles captivated my attention and arrested my imagination. The characters that relied on the invisible God and reaped tangible rewards began to motivate me. And these teachings exposed areas of my heart that otherwise would have continued to live in egotistic irresponsibility.

I know that it has been said before, but the book began reading me as I read it. Not only was I learning about God's nature, I was also learning about myself. Sometimes it brought elation and other times it made me uncomfortable, but I recognized what God was doing. He was using my holy habit to prepare me to fulfill my destiny.

"He was using my holy habit to prepare me to fulfill my destiny."

Can You Hear Me?

One day while in the sanctuary at my church, I saw an opportunity to have some fun with a young boy. While getting some things ready in the sound booth, I noticed little Michael playing on the stage. So taking a microphone, I began to whisper, *"Michael… Michael, can you hear me?"*

Looking around with a cute, confused look on his face, he nodded. *"Michael, it's me, God. I am in the box."* (Don't you think it is time we let God out of the box?)

Quickly, Michael took three steps over to the monitor that was sitting on the stage and gazed in as if he were peering into a deep hole. *"Michael, can you see me?"* With an innocent expression, he nodded.

"I am waving at you. Why aren't you waving back?"

Although he did not speak, Michael gave me the response I had hoped for. Without hesitation, he began to wave into the box.

By this time, I was struggling to contain my laughter. This little boy had not yet learned cynicism. With purity in his heart, he was listening to the voice of "God" and responding in obedience. (Don't worry, I have already asked forgiveness for my prank.)

A similar experience became the defining moment for Samuel—only the voice speaking to him did not come from a deranged authority figure that received joy from playing pranks on people younger than himself. It came directly from Heaven.

"Samuel, Samuel."

The voice came in the middle of the night as Samuel lay in the temple. He thought the voice was coming from Eli. Quickly, he got up and ran to his mentor. *"What do you need, Eli?"*

Not realizing what was happening, Eli told him that he had not called him. *"You must be hearing things. Go back and lie down."*

However, shortly after returning to where he was lying, the voice came again. *"Samuel, Samuel."*

Again, he ran toward Eli, trying to discover what was needed. *"I did not call you. Go back and lie down."*

Again, the voice came. *"Samuel, Samuel."*

One more time, Samuel jumped up from where he was resting and ran to the priest. *"You called?"*

It took three times before the priest understood what was going on. *"Samuel, I am not the one calling you. I believe it is the Lord."* After a short pause that allowed the severity of the sentence to sink in, Eli continued. *"Go back and lie down. When the Lord calls out again, you must answer him. Say, 'Speak, Lord, for your servant is listening.'"*

Can you imagine what must have been going through this young man's mind? He had given his life to serving the spiritual leaders of the nation, but he never had aspirations that one day he might be speaking to the Lord of the nation. When Eli enlightened him to whom the caller was, he must have been anxious. *"What does he want with me? Why would he be calling out in the middle of the night?"* Although he had more questions than answers, he decided that he was going to take Eli's advice. If God had chosen to speak to him, he was going to respond appropriately.

Lying down in the same spot that he had three times vacated to find Eli, he did not dare close his eyes. The pace of his heart made it a challenge to remain still and motionless, but the expectation that something remarkable was going to happen held him captive.

When his name was called, he awkwardly responded just as Eli had instructed. *"Speak, Lord, you servant is listening."* At this, the conversation began. The life-altering relationship between a young boy and the mighty Counselor was established. Samuel's preparation was in full swing.

As the priestly apprentice portioned out time to be with God, he was not simply learning *about* him, he was discovering his character, understanding his heart, and getting glimpses of his plan. As he learned to listen to his voice, he was being shaped and sculpted. He was being equipped and prepared for leadership. Samuel was being primed for responsibility.

"As the priestly apprentice portioned out
time to be with God, he was not simply
learning about him, he was discovering
his character, understanding his heart,
and getting glimpses of his plan."

If Samuel had not returned to the place where he was lying down and waited for the heavenly voice, God would have had to look elsewhere to discover a man who would faithfully lead. Had he not learned to listen, history would have been very different.

But he did return. He did listen. And he willingly obeyed. Because Samuel was a listener, God made him a prophet. Because he was a servant, God made him a leader. Because he was familiar with God's presence, God introduced him to his power. He was consecrated to God at an early age, but when positioned in the presence of holiness, he was confiscated by God to influence history.

Whether he knew what was transpiring or not, we do not know. However, it was the time set apart to sit with God, listen to his voice, and soak in his presence that gave God permission to move him toward his destiny. It was his righteous obsession and holy habit that moved him toward his revolutionary lifestyle.

Samuel learned that the foundation for all victories is laid before the battle begins. It is in his presence that God inspires faith, courage, and wisdom. God builds warriors in private before he releases them in public. He shapes them in secret before the battles begin.

Chapter Two

Before The Battle Begins

Thought For The Day:

> If you give God some time daily, He
> will change your forever.

Scripture Theme:

> James 4:8 "Come near to God and he will come near to you."

Questions To Ponder:

> What will you do when God speaks to you?
>
> Are you heart challenged by Samuel's habit
> of pursuing God's presence? What action can
> you do today that would build such a habit?
>
> What are the main hindrances or attitudes that
> keep you from spending time with God?

Digging Deeper:

> The beginning of Samuel's life and
> ministry is recorded in 1 Samuel 1–3.

CHAPTER 3

Integrity: Who Are You—Really?

Using the same line of questioning about sin that is asked about a tree in the forest, let me pose a query. *"If a sin is committed, but there is no one around to see it, is it really a sin?"*

This has been an issue I have dealt with since I was a child. I always thought that if I could cover up my disobedience, hiding it from my parents and other authority figures, then my disobedience had not been severe. Let me tell you how this affected my behavior growing up.

Much to the dismay of my mother, I entered into my teen years with an overwhelming addiction to sugar. I craved it in all its delicious forms—couldn't get enough. Candy whispered sweetly—inviting me to indulge: candy bars, gummy bears, Pixie Sticks, Junior Mints, peanut butter cups, Tootsie Rolls, Blow Pops, Pezz, Skittles (I could go on forever). Baked goods called out to me: cookies, pies, cakes, and pastries. Even the manufactured counterfeits that were available from Hostess and Little Debbie had a tractor beam hold: from Zingers to Twinkies.

I could be easily seduced by the dilly bars at Dairy Queen, the soft ice cream available through the McDonald's drive-through, or any of the thirty-one flavors available under the pink banner of Baskin and Robins.

When not available in the creatively prepared and deliciously yummy versions listed above, I would find my sugar in raw forms, either through handfuls of sweet cereals or in fingers full of the pure cane—did you know that if you lick your finger and stick it into the sugar bowl, the white stuff sticks?

However, there was one treat I enjoyed more than any other. My all-time favorite was the Mars Bar: A flawless delicacy to be sure. But one that got me into trouble once when I was a freshman in high school.

It was a Monday afternoon when my mom and I found ourselves at the grocery store near our home.

As we entered, I sensed the candy aisle calling my name. Although it was my mom who had the list, I had an agenda. I wanted a Mars Bar. But I knew that I should not be the one to bring up the idea.

Whenever I would out-right ask for sugar, a defense mechanism in my mother would react and shoot down my suggestion as if it were a scud missile perfectly on target. So, instead of bringing up the candy aisle, I silently prayed that Mom would respond to the candy's loneliness. I put on my sweetest expression—the one I employed when I wanted something.

When my mom turned down the proper aisle, I thought I heard the "Hallelujah Chorus" rise from out of nowhere. When she began to place handfuls (my mother was always a bargain shopper and she usually purchased in bulk) of Mars Bars into her cart, I wanted to do back flips. But I tried to play it cool, looking like I was unaware my mom had counted 12 candy bars.

My mom was the best. I prepared my impromptu speech of acceptance with which I would receive my candy bar as soon as we got into the car. *"Mom, I didn't see you get these. You shouldn't have. I really don't need any candy today...Well, OK, if you insist."* I was going to be smooth.

But as my mom began to load the groceries into the trunk, she did not offer me one. Perhaps she was waiting until we got home. But I did not get one there either.

As I emptied the trunk and carried the groceries inside the house, my mom picked up the plastic bag containing the 12 bars and disappeared into her room. In a few minutes, she returned…but without the bag.

Although I kept silent, inside, I was getting angry. I felt as if she had led me on. She brought me up to the mountain of expectancy and then violently threw me off the cliff leaving me disappointed, disillusioned, and hungry…and, slightly bitter. Not only had she failed to offer me a candy bar…she hid them from me.

As I lay in bed that night, I could not drift off to sleep. All I could think about were those candy bars that rightfully belonged to me—that wanted to be with me—that were being held hostage just a few feet away.

As I awoke in the morning, thoughts of the injustice had disappeared. After grabbing a bowl of sugary cereal (the only way for a young man to begin a hyperactive day), I headed off to school.

Hours later, I returned to the house and discovered there was no one there. My mom, for reasons I can no longer remember, was not home. My dad was at work. My brother had gone home with a friend. I was all alone—except for those Mars Bars.

Something inside reminded me I was not to go into their room without permission, but the simultaneous voices of 12 candy bars echoed louder throughout the house.

I wish I could say that I put up some semblance of a fight, but I did not. I gave in to the urge—the compulsion to seek out their hiding place. I convinced myself that I would be able to embezzle one candy bar without anyone knowing. I ignored my conscience (or was that the Holy Spirit) reminding me I should respect my parents' wishes.

It did not take me long to discover the stash of candy my mother was hiding from me. It was in her favorite hiding place. The one place she was convinced no squirrelly 14-year-old would dare to look out of sure embarrassment. It was in her underwear drawer.

Right there, underneath all of her silk pretties, lay the plastic bag from the night before. In that bag was the prize. To be honest, I was uncomfortable digging through that particular drawer. However, I was fixated on the immediate satisfaction that would come if and when I uncovered the reserve.

I did not have much time to ponder my next move. Following my discovery, I heard the garage door begin to open. My mom was home.

The need to make a decision was pressing. I could replace the bag, shut the drawer, and leave the room; or, I could grab a bar and make my exit.

I chose the second option. With a Mars Bar in hand, I ran into the restroom and locked the door.

"Sean, are you home?"

With my mom in the house, I quickly opened the wrapper and inhaled the candy bar. I did not enjoy it; heck, I ate it so fast, I did not even taste it.

"Yeah Mom, I'm in the bathroom," came my reply.

Guilt was not even a consideration at that point. I did not regret sneaking around or stealing. But I did have a strong apprehension to getting caught. So, I dug to the bottom of the garbage and buried the wrapper.

As I left the bathroom, I felt confident. Not that I had done the right thing…but that I had covered up the wrong things I had done. I was sure I had gotten away with it. I did not think about it the rest of the night. I would not have thought about it for the rest of my life, had my plan not been altered.

"As I left the bathroom, I felt confident. Not that I had done the right thing…but that I had covered up the wrong things I had done."

Remember, the candy bars were purchased on Monday. I stole one and gulped it and tried to hide the evidence on Tuesday...and I was discovered and humiliated on Wednesday.

Wednesdays were my favorite days growing up. The main reason was because that was the night we had youth group. But another reason was that was when Donna and Cindy came home with my brother.

My brother was a year older than me, and so were his friends. Every Wednesday my brother would bring home two of the most attractive girls in his class. They would hang out with us in the afternoon, then go to church with us in the evening.

Because I had a crush on these beauties (realistically, I had a crush on every girl who was kind, sweet, and would give me the time of day), I loved being around them. Because they were a little older than me, I worked hard to come off as mature and intelligent. It almost never worked (I always stuck my foot in my mouth), but this particular day, my immaturity was truly exposed.

When the four of us entered the house after school, Mom greeted us in her normal fashion. A snack of cookies and milk waited for us on the kitchen table. As we began to dig into Mom's famous monster cookies, I tried to get involved in the conversation, but what I saw hanging on the refrigerator stole my ability to speak.

"I tried to get involved in the conversation, but what I saw hanging on the refrigerator stole my ability to speak."

There, taped to the door, was the Mars Bar wrapper I had tried to dispose of. After a few minutes of trying to ignore my impending doom, my mother took the wrapper off the door and without speaking, placed it on the table in front of me.

With Donna and Cindy looking on, my brother asked, "*What's this?*"

Trying to sound innocent, with a shaky voice, I chirped, "*Yeah, what's this?*"

My mother looked at me for about 10 seconds (seemed like an eternity), then asked, "*Sean, you don't know anything about this?*"

Although my goose was cooked and I knew it, I lied. But after two minutes of that gaze, followed by mild interrogation, sweat started to pour from my body. I was trying to hold it together because Donna and Cindy were watching, but the pure emotion and humiliation got the best of me. I burst into tears and confessed my guilt.

I think my mother operated on the premise that she could humiliate all rebellion out of me—so with my tears flowing, she took it further. *"Sean, where did you get this Mars Bar?"*

Sensing the direction she was taking, I begged her not to go there, but she would have none of it. *"Sean, where was it?"*

"Mom, please don't."

"Sean, where was the candy bar?"

I whispered, *"In your room."*

"Where in my room, Sean?"

Sheepishly I replied, *"In your dresser."*

"Which drawer?"

Glancing across the table and seeing the girls' eyes bigger than usual, I tried to avoid the inevitable. *"The third one, Mom."*

"What do I keep in my third drawer, Sean?"

She wasn't going to give up until all this was out in the open.

I did not say these next words. I blurted them out along with a humiliating waterfall of tears. *"Your underwear."*

(Actually, the story stops when I first burst into tears, but looking back, it would have been funnier if she had pressed the issue.)

What a Strange Question

Because this horrible experience is years behind me, I can now laugh. But at the time, I could not. That day, I could barely breathe, let alone find the humor in my stupidity and circumstances. I was humiliated—and I was convinced the tag "*perverted boy who plays with his mom's silk things*" was going to haunt me for the rest of my school days—if not the rest of my life.

This moment of poor judgment has given me a lot of perspective on the misconceptions I had about right and wrong, about righteousness and sin. Much of my life has been spent trying to get away with sin, thinking if I hide it well enough and if I cover it up cleverly enough, then there will be no immediate consequences.

"Because I understand that God wants a consistent life of godliness and integrity from me, I desire to be the same person behind closed doors and I am in front of others."

Sometimes I have been good at cloaking it, and other times (as in the case with the Mars Bar), I have not. But thankfully, my perspectives have changed. I no longer am satisfied trying to cover up my weak will and disobedience. Because I understand that

God wants a consistent life of godliness and integrity from me, I desire to be the same person behind closed doors as I am in front of others.

Although it took me a while to learn the lesson and adopt it into my lifestyle, I now know that God cares a great deal about character and integrity. He really does.

This life of faith is not to be one of false perceptions and polished masks in public while living chaotic lifestyles of selfish indulgence when no one is around. The warrior's life (although we will not be perfect) is to be one of sincerity, honesty, consistent growth, selflessness, and sin avoidance. That is, after all, the moral to one of the strangest stories in Scripture.

In Genesis 32, God went out for a walk and ended up ambushing a guy sitting by the fire. After they wrestled all night, God threw his hip out of socket, and then asked him who he was. Odd, don't you think? Let's check it out.

With the cool of the night nipping at his face, Jacob sat warming himself by the fire. As the sparks danced and the smoke rose, it did not illuminate the image standing by the trees. Nervous about the morning reunion with his twin brother whom he had not seen in over 20 years, but unaware of the threat just a few feet away, he pondered his life.

Deceit, manipulation, and duplicity had defined Jacob's relationships, and self-preservation had motivated him. I would say these things had ruined his friendship with his brother, but that would indicate that at one time they had some sort of bond—not the case. From the time of conception, a war had waged...turns out these twins were not on great terms even before they had opened eyes or exercised lungs.

During the pregnancy, they fought in their mother's womb, and the birth was suspect as Esau came out first—but not by five or ten minutes—by seconds. Jacob arrived *"on his heels"* as they say—literally grasping it.

As they grew, the conflict was constant and the bickering routine. Esau dished it out to the momma's boy who loved to cook, clean, and felt most comfortable in his mother's company. In return, Jacob teased Esau about his appearance (when he was born, he looked *"like a hairy garment"* Genesis 25:25) and his name (Esau literally means *"Hairy"*).

The two brothers could not have been more different—nor could they have been more malicious.

One day, Jacob convinced Esau to sell his birthright for nothing more than a bowl of stew, only to turn around a few years later and trick their blind father into granting the inheritance and blessing that belonged to Esau, to the younger son. When his mother learned that Esau intended to harm her favorite son, she convinced him to tuck tail and run.

When Jacob left, he was a poor man running out of fear for his life. Now, he readies to return with wives, children, livestock, and an apology to make.

That is when it happened. That is when the story turns strange. Without a whisper of warning, someone pounced. A pile driver caught Jacob off guard and pinned him to the ground.

What would you do if someone—something—jumped you in the dark of night and wrestled you to the ground? You would try to get away, wouldn't you?—That is exactly what Jacob did. With aggressive movements intended to free himself from the assailant's hold, he kicked and squirmed, hoping, if nothing else, to get a glance at the face of his attacker.

Questions raced through his mind. *"Who is this?" "Why is he attacking me?" "Is he alone, or are there others?" "Could it be Esau come to repay me for the ways I wronged him years ago?"*

But as the struggle continued, he realized this was not Esau—it was like no one he had met before. The strength was abnormal—superhuman. He worked relentlessly to escape, thinking if he could just break his grip, he may have a shot at disappearing into the woods. But that was a meaningless pursuit.

At times, Jacob felt as if he was being toyed with instead of assaulted. He sensed that his enemy was holding back—that he could hurt him, or even kill him, any moment he desired to. This frightening sensation made him fight even harder.

Each passing hour, Jacob seemed to lose steam. He was tiring; only the adrenaline enhanced by fear kept him anxiously and energetically trying to break free. The battle continued—until night gave way to morning.

As the sun began to peak over the mountains, the encounter took an interesting turn. Intentionally, an index finger made its way towards Jacob's hip. After wrestling for hours, Jacob and the mysterious stranger had bumped, scratched, clawed, elbowed, kicked, pinched, and hit each other, but this time, one strategic touch changed their encounter.

Something locked up. When the finger touched the hip, it froze. The joint became immobile. Jacob knew from the beginning he would never forget the encounter, but after the touch—that strange and powerful touch to his hip, he knew this midnight tussle would forever define him.

Sensing he was in the presence of divinity, he stopped trying to escape. Manipulating his damaged hip, he turned and grabbed hold of the man who had touched him.

"I won't let go until you bless me."

Curious was the reply, *"What is your name?"*

Strange, don't you think? After wrestling through the night and exhibiting mercy by not driving Jacob into the dirt and returning him to dust, God asks his name.

But why? Why would God want to know the name of the person He is wrestling? Had God gone out for exercise one night, and in a moment of obnoxious playfulness, jumped the first guy He found alone by a campfire? Did He not know who He was fighting against?

No...that is not the reason He asked for a name. He was not asking for information (God knows all things—He certainly knew it was Jacob He was rustling with that night). He was asking for a confession.

You see, back in biblical times, names were not simply labels—they were definitions. A name did not offer a designation; it told people WHO you were—and WHAT. When God asked Jacob for a name, He was saying, *"Ok, Jacob, I want you to tell me who you are, how you live your life, and what you see when you look in the mirror."*

The question hit Jacob like a strong jab to the jaw. *"In shock of realization, whispering, he said 'Jacob—supplanter, schemer, trickster, swindler!'"* (Genesis 32:27, Amplified).

He stopped fighting altogether in that moment. The question had pierced his conscience and illuminated all the crooked, crazy, and deceitful things he had done in his life. For the first time, he took an inventory of who he was, how he treated people, and the way he lived his life, and he did not like the image staring back in the mirror.

Stripped of all arrogance to the point where he could not even muster the energy to speak at normal volume, he confessed, *"I am a liar…"* *"I am dishonest…"* *"I stole from my brother…"* *"I lied to my father…"* *"I manipulated my uncle…"*

Although God had refused to destroy him as they wrestled, His questioning was not as merciful. With that one question echoing through his mind, his façade faded. He could not cover up his weak integrity.

"Although God had refused to destroy him as they wrestled, His questioning was not as merciful."

The finger of God had touched his hip and created a life-altering limp. Then with one question, He pierced his heart, withdrew a confession, and began to change his identity. *"That is who you were—no longer. You will no longer be the Jacob of old who manipulates, deceives, and acts selfishly. I am remaking you to be Israel* (God actually renamed him on the spot). *You will fight for Me and for My purposes."*

Integrity Matters

In the past, I have accepted character flaws in my life and used manipulative tactics to get my own way. I have perfected the art of covering up my weaknesses. And I have run from consequences rather than accept responsibility. Because I have become so accustomed to my self-indulgences and willingly embraced my petty behaviors, I have ignored conviction. However, like Jacob, I have also had encounters with Christ where He asked my name.

In those moments, I am completely aware that I am an open book. God does not need information about my life; he knows everything about me. He knows the choices I have made, the attitudes I have embraced, and the level of my obedience. He is looking for a confession.

With the presence of God resting heavy on me, and His Spirit peering deeply into my soul, I have stopped the charade and professed my guilt. *"God, I am a liar…I am a thief…I am selfish…I am arrogant."* (Sometimes these encounters last for days.)

Those moments are always hard, but they have proven to be monumental to my development. They are stepping stones to stronger character. Those offerings of honest confession and true repentance have given God the opportunity to change my name. *"That is what you were…but I am transforming you. You were a liar, but I am making you an ambassador for truth. You were a manipulator, but I am granting you the ability to love purely with no concern for what you receive in return. You struggle with pride, but I am going to convince you that it is about me."*

As someone with a selfish streak, I dread those encounters. But as a warrior who wants to be a man of integrity, I am willing to embrace them.

Chapter Three

Who Are You Really?

Thought For The Day:

> If God was to ask you - "Who are you?"
> How would you respond?

Scripture Theme:

> 1 John 1:9 "If we confess our sins, he is faithful and just and
> will forgive us our sins and purify us from all unrighteousness."

Questions To Ponder:

> Do you like who you are when you
> think no one else is looking?
>
> Would you care if all your secrets were
> revealed for the world to see?
>
> Are you running from consequences
> rather than accepting responsibility?

Digging Deeper:

> The story of God and Jacob's wrestling
> match is found in Genesis 32:22-32.

CHAPTER 4

Excuses: Learning To Trust

The call goes out to would-be warriors, *"Come and make war: Fight for justice. Spread the truth. Resist the evil one. Populate heaven and decimate hell."*

But instead of responding in courage to the invitation, excuses are the first things that come to mind. Rather than boldly declaring, *"If God is for me who can be against me,"* a pathetic trickle ensues. Oh, it is not that we don't want to be used to wield the flag of the Almighty—we do. We fear being over-looked as God gathers his army and instigates a revolt against the secular culture that either neglects God or rejects him. We daydream about being vessels of righteousness and blazing weapons in God's arsenal; however, our response reveals that those desires are overpowered.

Failing to understand that God can overcome our imperfection and fill the void revealed by our weaknesses, we try to convince God that we are not right for the job. *"Lord, are you sure you have the right guy? I mean, maybe in a couple of years I will be ready to live against the culture and speak what is unpopular, but truthfully, I am not ready yet...I have only been a Christian for a short time...I don't know the Bible well enough...I haven't prayed through..."*

Although the excuses are as numerous as the grains of salt in a shaker, they all center around one theme: We do not trust God. Impulsively, we react as if God's vision is limited and his understanding vague—as if he knows some things, but not all. In those moments, we treat him as if he were only our Savior, failing to recognize that he is also our knowledgeable Creator, and removing from him the title and authority he has as our supreme Leader.

"Impulsively, we react as if God's vision is limited and his understanding vague—as if he knows some things, but not all."

Immediate obedience is the only reaction that makes sense for willing warriors. However, most days that is not my first response. Because I stare in the mirror of my inadequacies more often than into the scope of his ability and will at work in me, I argue...I debate...I make excuses.

A Strange Messenger

God speaks to me in strange ways. I know of many people who have experienced prophetic visions and dreams—not me. The majority of the times in my life when I have had a personal revelation or a spiritual epiphany they have been revealed through strange means, and sometimes curious messengers. Such was the case in the late summer of 1989.

While moving from Northern California to Colorado to pursue an open door the Lord provided in ministry, I had an encounter—a visitation that continues to influence me. This visitation that I speak of was not with a prophetic man or a righteous woman of God who inspired me with wisdom, discernment, or counsel. I did not slip into a trance and visit some celestial place. Neither did I envision an illuminated angelic being that spoke of unknown mysteries. No—as strange as it sounds, the messenger that day was a simple seagull.

Sitting in my rented Ryder truck through desolate portions of Nevada on Interstate 70, the activity around me slowed down to a crawl. As if it was happening in slow motion, I saw a white bird come into my view several yards in front of my vehicle. Because time had decelerated, I noticed everything in the landscape and every detail on that bird. Now, you might think I am making this up, but as the bird began to cross my path, I saw him cock his head to look straight at me…then he smiled. He was deliberate with his expression because he knew what was about to happen.

With that sly smile on his little beak, he unleashed the largest load of bird doo-doo ever recorded in the history of bird-dom. It hit my windshield like a sheet of a dozen paintballs splattering against their target. The barrage was not limited to my window. A large portion of my yellow truck was now white. Because it happened in slow motion and I saw the bird smile (I stand by my story), I began to laugh out loud. The attack hit me as humorous.

Wanting to clear my windshield of all that had landed there, I quickly reached for my wiper controls only to discover that this particular truck had exhausted the healthy life of its blades. Instead of clearing the milky substance from the glass, the wipers simply pushed it back and forth, smearing it with each stroke. Again…laughter.

After a few minutes spent gazing through the diluted (but now dried) film on my window, something caught my attention. Positioned directly in front of me was a colorful speck—a chunk, if you will, that obviously had come from the seagull.

Because I am a strange (sometimes deranged) person who has a unique perspective on life and is unafraid to ask curious questions, a thought popped into my brain that I could not ignore (please don't judge me). Looking at this green mass, I asked myself, "*I wonder what he had for lunch?*"

Now, I know that is sick, but hang with me. My curiosity led me to an interesting revelation—not about the diet or dining habits of Nevada's seafowl, but about myself. Concentrating my focused attention on that chunk, I lost sight of all other things in my picture. The windshield became hazy, the road blurred, and the terrain disappeared from my view. All I could see was the object that I was converging on. And that almost got me into trouble.

I began to drift in the road—actually, off the road. My yellow Ryder truck was heading for the ditch until I recognized the rumble marks on the road beneath me (driving by brail is sometimes effective). I sat back in my seat and again, found the center of the road.

Being slow to learn from my mistakes, after a few minutes my curiosity returned, and I leaned toward the dropping again. Same habit, same result. The rumbling woke me to my position in the road.

As I sat back up in my seat (with slight laughter still in my heart) God spoke to me. In that gentle whisper I have come to know and love (aren't you glad he doesn't shout and scream?), he said, *"See how easy to distract you are?"*

In that moment, I understood something about myself. *I have a focus problem.* I realized that in my truck, my perception was affected by what I chose to look at. When I sat back in my chair and looked past the mess on my windshield, I barely noticed it was there. Although it wanted to hinder my view and distract my focus, it did not affect me in any way.

However, when I focused on the mass in front of me, all other things faded. The road seemed to disappear. The sunshine became insignificant. And the signs that were intended to offer direction had no impact. I realized my lesson that day was not about driving but about me.

There are times in my life when all is good, yet I focus on things that are distractions or that steal my confidence. I see everything that I am not instead of everything that God is and what he has promised I can become. I can lose focus. Even when the Son is shining on me, the road is beckoning me forward, and destiny is in view, I have a sick ability to lean forward to study a problem in my life or a weakness that exists until I begin to drift off my course.

I have been known to stare at the smudge on my windshield that looks identical to unsightly inconsistencies in my character, and instead of leading me to correct that flaw and move on toward

God's plan, my focus has forced me to argue with God when he sends me an assignment rather than go in the confidence that he has forgiven me and that he will continue to work through me. There have been times when I have been consumed with my lack of experience or knowledge rather than trust God to work through my frailties and keep trucking toward my God-prescribed destination.

In my life, when I have converged on my problems instead of his greatness, I have offered excuses. I have squabbled with him, telling him why I was not the right person or why this wasn't the right time. But, looking back, I have never won any of those arguments. I have never caught him off guard with some piece of the puzzle that he missed, some source of information that he overlooked, or some angle that inspired him to change his choice. With a patient smile, he has simply waited for me to willfully trust and submit.

Sometimes these issues of focus have lasted a few short minutes or days, and I come to my senses as I hear the rumblings of inactivity. Other times, they last months. Instead of drifting in the road, I have detoured off the path or even wound up in the ditch stalled, frustrated, and confused—watching the activity of purpose on the streets nearby but unable or too afraid to step in.

Excuses are barriers *I* construct (formed because of misinformation) that keep me from fulfilling my desire to be used. They are not vision-altering, call-inhibiting, and victory-limiting revelations that affect my future—unless I cling to them.

"Excuses are barriers *I* construct (formed because of misinformation) that keep me from fulfilling my desire to be used."

So often we give God our excuses of why he can't use us or others. We see these excuses like a protective tower that shields us from the pain of failure, but in the end, it becomes a jail cell keeping us from the freedom of victory in Christ; The victory that comes when we see our calling and come out of hiding.

Me?...Are you Kidding?

Gideon was hiding. So why did God choose him? He was not perfecting his skill with the sword, honing his ability with the bow, enlisting soldiers to fight for the cause, or working on a strategy for an attack—he was holed up, hoping *not* to be discovered. So why was he recruited?

Why did God select this man—this terrified man—to lead an assault? He was God's first choice because fear wasn't the only emotion he was harboring.

For seven years, the oppressors had oppressed. God's people had been bullied in their own country. The land and the people had been molested. All of the Israelites had accepted their plight. They wrote off freedom as a luxury no longer available and not worth fighting for.

But in Gideon, something was beginning to stir. He was becoming uncomfortably uneasy. Anger was boiling right next to the fear. With the memories of injustices still fresh in his mind, he pictured the faces that had stolen livestock, looted homes, or burned villages. Another picture in his mind was those of family members and friends whose lives had been ravaged due to the siege. His mild irritation had simmered for months; it was turning into an antagonized rage. The very thought of the enemy infuriated him. Perhaps he was angry with himself as well. Like the time I watched a "jock" pick a fight with a "geek" and did nothing, perhaps he was frustrated with his fear and mad that he had remained paralyzed.

Although he had been held captive and avoided the confrontation, Gideon was not satisfied with inactivity. He knew there was a reason to fight back, but his mind and heart had not yet agreed on the means to do so. He had heard stories about God's provision, protection, and miraculous ability to defeat the armies of the past—he believed it with his mind, but his heart could not embrace the faith necessary to come out of hiding and engage the enemy.

"He knew there was a reason to fight back, but his mind and heart had not yet agreed on the means to do so."

The thought of the would-be attack brought a smile to his face. Because he had limited experience as a man of war, he was not sure if he could succeed against the enemies' army. But in his pictures, he always tasted victory. That is why God chose and recruited Gideon: because he was angry at the injustice and he dreamt of being part of the answer.

"The Lord is with you, mighty warrior."

Gideon was caught off guard by this odd greeting. First of all, he did not know the stranger and was concerned that his hiding place had been compromised. But it also seemed strange since the one hiding and dreaming, but refusing to fight, was referred to as a warrior.

Rather than accept the prophetic greeting that was personal and meant only for him, Gideon manipulated it in his mind as he failed to recognize the moment of individual affirmation that was taking place. *"If the Lord is with US, why has all this happened to us? Where are all his wonders that our fathers told us about...?"*

However, the Lord would not be distracted. *"Go in the strength you have and save Israel out of Midian's hand. Am I not sending you?"*

Sirens went off in his head. He began to argue with himself and with God. *"Me?...You want me to save Israel? Are you kidding? Don't you know that I am the weakest link in the least influential family? I am not the man that you are looking for."*

The Lord would not be deterred. He knew that if Gideon would get his eyes off of his shortcomings and limitations, the desire for justice inside of him would drive him to victory. He was the right man. This was the right time.

However, the smudge on his windshield was keeping him from believing—from trusting. All he could see was his lack of experience amplified by his fear, his lack of influence intensified by his insecurity, and his weakness magnified by his failures. Rather than accepting his charge and running to the battle with confidence, he argued. He made excuses.

But God answered: *"I will be with you, and you will strike down all of the Midianites together."*

Unspoken thoughts of hope began to percolate. *"Could it be? Could God really be calling me to the battle?"*

After a series of fleece tests that the struggling-to-believe Gideon insisted upon, his faith was beginning to grow. Fear still existed, but trust was budding and belief blooming. So he acted. Through sacrifice, he established his allegiance to God. Then he lashed out at the false gods that were dominating the culture. He tore down the idols and crushed the altars.

This created quite a stir with the people who were still loyal to these practices. They angrily approached seeking retribution but he escaped unharmed. His dad saved him with simple logic. *"Listen, if Baal is really a god, he can handle his own business."*

When it came time to gather an army, Gideon must have wandered back into his insecurity. *"What if no one comes?"* But come they did. Thousands came out when they heard that someone with a warrior's courage was assembling soldiers. From an army of one to a gathering of over 32,000 within days—in the same time, Gideon changed from a self-proclaimed weak link to a commander who was becoming inflated.

Gideon's pride was growing. As he saw the plan of God come together, he started to enjoy the leadership that he had been given. He enjoyed the charge of *"General"* that he received as he walked among the troops. As each moment passed, his ego increased.

So God decided to let some air out of Gideon's balloon.

"You have too many here. I can't deliver them into your hands. Because the army is great, you will not rely on my might. You will go to battle with arrogant strategies. Gideon, send some home."

Confused at the request, yet aware that obedience was required, he told anyone who was afraid of battle to return to their wives and children. In the morning the army boasted an impressive 32,000 soldiers; in the evening it had dropped to only 10,000. God, however, was not shocked by the situation.

"That's OK," thought Gideon. *10,000 isn't bad. I would rather have 10,000 who are unafraid and ready to war than 32,000 who are timid."* But as he began to formulate plans for the attack, he did not involve God.

So, much to Gideon's dismay, God dismissed almost the entire army. Only 300 remained after God had selected his arsenal, using their drinking habits at the brook as his barometer.

"300? Are you kidding me? God, you are sending me to fight this vast army—to bring deliverance to Israel—to defeat the tyranny with only 300?"

Yet, God had chosen. He wanted the strategy to reflect his wisdom—the kind of wisdom that confounds the wise. Thousands would clutter the process, but a few hundred would ensure that Gideon and all the kingdoms of the world would know that it was because of God's might that the oppressors were punished.

But with only 300 men in the camp, Gideon (and I am sure some of the soldiers) experienced anxiety. *"Gideon,"* God commanded, *"sneak down into the camp of the enemy. I want to convince you once and for all that as long as you are fighting for me, nothing can stand in your way."*

So on an expedition in search of courage, Gideon crept toward the tents of God's enemies. When he arrived, he heard a bedside conversation about a dream. Prophetically, it was interpreted mentioning Gideon as the one who would crush this immense army.

Now he was ready. He snuck down the hill trying not to be heard, but he boldly ran up it. Barging into the camp of his 300 knights, he roused them from sleep and said, *"It is time. Take a trumpet in one hand and a jar, which hides a lamp in the other* (not the typical weapons of war). *We are going to surround the hill. When we get there, watch me. Do what I do and shout, 'For the Lord and for Gideon.'"*

The one that the Lord had recruited because he was angry at the injustice and wanted to be a part of the revolution watched as the Lord inspired chaos in that camp. With trumpets blaring, voices rising, and lamps shining, the heathen soldiers turned on each other and began to kill one another. The ones who escaped the Lord's ambush were tracked down by the Israelites who had come out of their towns to pursue. In one swift move, God brought deliverance and restored freedom. And he chose to use an insignificant, fearful, yet hopeful man to lead the charge.

Once he got past his excuses and he resolved to trust in the only one who can bring victory in impossible circumstances, he began to enjoy the responsibility that he had been given and the mandate that had been placed upon his life. However, he did have to let God destroy his excuses. If he had held onto them, history would read very differently. Gideon would not be listed among the judges and deliverers of Israel.

Had he not looked past the smudges of insecurity, irrelevance, and weakness that had strategically been placed on the prominent windshield of his life, he would not have discovered his destiny.

Beyond the Excuses

My heart is consumed with anger at the injustices that occur in our society. Hypocrisy, abuse, and manipulative tactics that damage lives and turn people skeptical irritate me every time I sense them. When I see the lies that permeate our culture, seducing people from the truth of holiness, I squirm. And when the media glorifies things that destroy trust and innocence, my blood boils.

"I long to see Christ bring peace to lives that live in fear, hope to those who are desperate, and value to those who are insecure; I pray that I would be one dispensing the medicine the world needs to cure it's ills."

However, my hatred of these things leads me to dream that God could use me to defeat them. I long to see Christ bring peace to lives that live in fear, hope to those who are desperate, and value to those who are insecure; I pray that I would be one dispensing the medicine the world needs to cure it's ills.

God put those desires in my heart, and he has chosen to use me in this way. I am, after all, his child. I am a joint heir with Jesus; everything he has is mine. I am an ambassador of his good news; I get to share his unconditional love and unlimited mercy. I am dangerous to all things ungodly, for *"greater is he that is in me, then he that is in the world."*

But these promises will never materialize as long as I offer up excuses. I must get past them. I must overcome them, and so must all would be warriors.

Chapter Four

Learning to Trust

Thought For The Day:

> God is Bigger than the Devil is Bad.

Scripture Theme:

> 2 Timothy 1:7 "For God did not give us a spirit of timidity, but a spirit of power, of love and of self discipline."

Questions To Ponder:

> Are you arguing, debating, or making excuses that reflect your lack of trust in God?
>
> Are your eyes too focused on your shortcomings and limitations?
>
> Is there anything that God has asked you to do that requires you to take action?

Digging Deeper:

> Judges 6 & 7 share the story of Gideon's unlikely rise to warrior status.

CHAPTER 5

Chosen: Handpicked For The Cause

Intentional.

Strategic.

Deliberate.

Premeditated.

That is the way God creates.

His designs are not random...they are calculated.

With the Kingdom in view, he knows what he is going to need. Whether it is a fiery preacher, a committed counselor, a gifted businessman, a phenomenal athlete, a loving mother, a skilled soldier, or an exceptional politician, God makes note and commits to building someone for the task.

With excitement burning in his heart and anticipation visible in his eyes, God enters the cosmic laboratory. With a long lab coat draped over his frame, he hurries along thrilled about his latest project. He does not rush because he lacks time—after all, he has the expanse of eternity at his disposal—but his swift movements and rapid pace can be attributed to the pleasure he feels as he considers his masterpiece.

With the perfect amount of personality, the proper measure of conviction, and the right gifts, the inventor creates. Taking into consideration the environment, the struggles, and the ambitions that await, the Master Creator pours in grace, patience, faith, and wisdom in the required amounts.

On the day of conception, he steps back and eyes his magnum opus. Knowing that not one thing is lacking and nothing is missing, he releases a masterpiece into the world.

This particular work of art has a face and a name (yours). It is dripping with destiny. This one is a world-changer. With a beating heart, functioning lungs, and a brain that has great capacity, the journey of life begins—but the course has already been set.

There is potential to realize, promise to discover. There are battles to fight, great prayers to pray, lives to influence, truths to speak, convictions to live out, and contributions to be made; but oddly enough, these things might go undone—if the masterpiece never embraces his call.

If God's creation doesn't understand that there is a reason that his heart beats, his lungs function, and his brain works, he might drift through life—and miss opportunities. If the one fearfully and wonderfully made doesn't recognize the intentions of his design, he will neglect his life's purpose and overlook his role in the Master's plan.

Warriors who make their mark on culture do so because they believe they are an intentional creation that God blessed with a calculated mix of gifts, talents, and perspectives. They realize they serve a specific purpose, and they give their lives to fulfill that call.

> **"Warriors who make their mark on culture do so because they believe they are an intentional creation that God blessed with a calculated mix of gifts, talents, and perspectives."**

Warriors understand that they were chosen and crafted to live great lives and do wonderful things as they represent the One who created them. This revelation gives them courage to stand out and confidence to speak up.

Chosen before Birth

He was not a conglomeration of random parts with no thought of who he would be or what he would do. Samson was specifically and intentionally crafted for a national cause. He was destined to be an historic figure before he nursed at his mother's breasts.

After 40 years of oppression, God could no longer silently observe the plight of his people. So, he crafted a plan.

He prepared a man—a warrior to lead a revolution. Prior to his conception, he was known. God miraculously opened the barren womb of a faithful woman and divinely inspired the inception of one man who would frustrate the plans of the Philistines while inspiring hope in the Israelites.

God could have sent a series of plagues to wipe out their enemies (he had, after all, done that before). An "Act of God" could have destroyed those extorting and enslaving them. But that was not the course of action he chose. He chose a man—even before he was a boy—to single handedly lead the revolution.

"In his infinite wisdom and creative genius, God fashions people for the tasks that lie ahead: to live counter to the culture, to pray reforming prayers, to speak freeing truth in the place of persecution, to authentically represent Christ to those who do not seek a spiritual voice."

This is still the method he uses to bring about change. In his infinite wisdom and creative genius, God fashions people for the tasks that lie ahead: to live counter to the culture, to pray reforming prayers, to speak freeing truth in the face of persecution, to authentically represent Christ to those who do not seek a spiritual voice.

God's got Skill, but do you have the Foundation?

God utilizes impeccable precision in the creation process. I know that I will never be confused with a handyman because as a human I may miss key steps when I build or craft something. God never does. When I consider my feeble efforts, I can't help but laugh at the miscues, but when I remember God's wonders, I am amazed.

God generously crafted the heavens, painted the landscapes, scooped out the oceans, and shaped the mountains. He created flowers, bushes, vines, and trees. Each has its own texture, aroma, beauty, and purpose. He fashioned insects that crawl, snakes that slither, birds that fly, kangaroos that bound, fish that swim, penguins that waddle, moles that burrow, and monkeys that swing. Each has its unique functions, sounds, and appeal.

Yet, in the midst of all that he shaped, the crown of his creation remains the human race. But not just the race as a whole—every person. Each one is unique, intentional, and serves a purpose. Every person was crafted to bring God pleasure, to play a role in the Kingdom Eternal, and to achieve every good purpose of God. God has given them everything they will need to achieve, but by their own lack of discipline, poor choices, or self-serving lifestyles, some people refuse to do the things that ensure a solid foundation and long-term success.

Samson's life might have fallen into this category. God's vision for Samson's life was amazing. I believe he envisioned a super warrior who would accomplish great things, defeat many enemies, and faithfully lead his people. Although that was his plan and his vision, the warrior's will would determine how effective he would be. Obedience would be key.

Through the prophetic announcement, Samson had been given some specific instructions about how he was to live his life. He was not to drink fermented drink, and he was not to cut his hair. When he began to ignore those instructions and follow his own pursuits, the erosion of his destiny began.

These principles do not only apply to muscle-bound forces of nature. They apply to all warriors who long to live on purpose and fulfill God's directives. The key to strength and success may not be in your hair or your drinking habits, but it will be found in obedience.

God has given every believer rules and regulations written in Scripture that will either ensure success or begin a landslide into the mire of mediocrity. These rules are not negotiable. God has listed them to show keys to a better life—a life close to God, saturated in power, and embedded in confidence.

Many of the instructions are discovered within the pages of Scripture. We are called to speak the truth, honor our parents, live selfless lives free from greed, and protect life. We are to hold onto Christ as our priority, embrace no other gods, and never speak the Lord's name flippantly. If we obey, we will experience God's blessings.

However, every warrior also is given another set of personal mandates. These are not written in God's Book as much as they are on the heart; and they are not for all believers, but they are specific to each person.

For some, God's plan may begin with them abstaining from dating. For others, he may give specific instructions about their entertainment. For others, the command that is tied into their effectiveness as a history maker can be found in their spiritual pursuits.

I will never forget the first time that I sensed God encouraging me to set time aside to fast on a regular basis. To be honest, I hate to fast, but I knew in that moment that the Lord wanted to use those times to both purge me and empower me. He wanted me to set aside food in order to discipline my body, open up my spirit, and reestablish my commitment to his Lordship and his plan.

At first I fought (depending on the day, I still do), but the prodding of his Spirit convinced me that this was key to my personal growth and the increase of my anointing.

Deciding to work up to my goal of regular three-day fasts, I chose to dedicate one day—a Thursday—to buffeting my body and drawing close to him.

It went great—for the first hour. But by 8:30 A.M., my body was screaming. My empty stomach was shouting obscenities in a growely language, and my energy level was incredibly low. By noon, my head had joined in and was throbbing—I am not sure if it was missing the nourishment or the caffeine, but by lunchtime, I had a major headache. In that moment, I began to argue with God—or should I say grumble.

I knew that the sacrifice I was making (giving up food for a day) was not monumental. I realized that it was miniscule compared to all that he had done for me, yet I was still disquieted. In the midst of the conscious struggle that was going on, I was aware that my hunger for the Lord was not what I had hoped it was. Instead of utilizing this day apart to draw close, hear his voice, experience his touch, and rest in him, all I could think about was food.

I wanted a burger, big and juicy. I was envisioning a 44 oz. coke (with extra caffeine). I was picturing hitting a drive-through (maybe more than one) and ordering everything that sounded good to me. Yet, in the midst of my conflict, I knew that the Lord had asked me to fast.

Well, that first fast ended well. By the end of the day, I had adequately recognized my tendencies and decided to crucify them on the altar of purpose. I knew that if I continued to live a shallow life built around food, entertainment, and social activity, I would live a frustrated faith defined by weak convictions and a powerless ministry. I chose to obey.

Since that day, I have learned to fast (as I have already stated, I don't always enjoy it). And I have discovered through obedience that fasting is the doorway through which God chooses to bless me, speak to me, inspire me, and encourage me.

He called me to fast. Not to punish me—rather, to equip me. The awareness that fasting would be a good discipline for me was not something I initiated or that I originally embraced. However, it has become one of the instructions that helped me lay the foundation for my life and ministry.

The Spirit of God will illuminate strategic directives to everyone who is willing to listen. And they will be as diverse as his intentions for their life. These commands will put the would-be warrior in strange company as he stands against the culture and lives by a different set of rules (remember how John the Baptist wore camel fur and ate locusts), but obedience is imperative.

The nudges of God's Spirit may seem insignificant and minor, but it is those nudges that lay the foundation for spiritual success. It is those Spirit-impressions that lead to a supernatural life.

"The nudges of God's Spirit may seem insignificant and minor, but it is those nudges that lay the foundation for spiritual success."

"Exactly"

There is one particular portion of Scripture that always reminds me that God's strategic and specific plan is played out in the little details of my life. It declares that God not only knows the place and exact time I live, but also the people whom I will come in contact with.

This Scripture professes that:

"From one man he made every nation of men, that they should inhabit the whole earth; and he determined the times set for them and the exact places where they should live.

God did this so that men would seek him and perhaps reach out for him and find him, though he is not far from each one of us." Acts 17:26–27

With anticipation in my heart, I can wake every morning knowing that my investment in that day was intended to be. God created me to dream aggressively, to pray with faith, and to live with conviction. He intended for me to run toward destiny, flee only from sin, and cooperate with him to accomplish preordained tasks.

"God created me to dream aggressively, to pray with faith, and to live with conviction."

There is a reason I am here. As a warrior, I know that if I trust God and embrace Divine intervention, I will be victorious.

Intentional.

Strategic.

Deliberate.

Premeditated.

That is the way God creates.

That is the way he fashioned me—and that is the way he crafted you.

We are warriors—handpicked for the cause.

Chapter Five Summary

Hand Picked For The Cause

Thought For The Day:

Every day you have a role to play, Prayers
to pray, and lives to influence.

Scripture Theme:

Acts 17: 26-27 "From one man he made every nation of
men, that they should inhabit the whole earth; and he determined
the times set for them and the exact places where they should live.
God did this so that men would seek him and perhaps reach out for
him and find him, though he is not far from each one of us."

Questions To Ponder:

Do you believe that God fashioned you with purpose?

Are you living in strict obedience to the guidelines
God has set up for your life no matter how
insignificant or minor those guidelines may seem?

Do you look at obedience as a way to worship a
loving God or a way to be tied down by a rule?

Digging Deeper:

Read Judges Chapter 13 to study
Samson's pronouncement and birth.

CHAPTER 6

Loneliness: A Warrior's Curse

Is it possible that a warrior unafraid to face any foe could be struck with a loneliness that saps his strength and will to fight?

Could solitude bring the courageous low?

Can isolation render the brave ineffective?

After having examined the lives of many personal heroes, I would have to say, "*Yes.*" Loneliness seems to be the ever-present companion of warriors and an invisible weapon that defies the defenses. A silent, invisible threat to champions of the faith, some of their most intense battles are fought against this personal demon. This disturbing companion of warriors has inspired many to take their focus off of the fight, withdraw from the battle, or hand in their armor all together.

At times in my own life, I've found it to be a paralyzing emotion poisoning my will and creating questions I struggle to answer. At one point in my faith-walk, I actually thought that if I was committed to Christ and dedicated to the cause, I would always be surrounded by a strong support system. I was under the impression that fellow believers in Christ would "have my back" as I stepped into uncharted territory with aggressive faith. However, that has not proven to be the case. Actually, the opposite has proven true.

In moments when I've ventured out furthest on a limb, not only have I felt unsupported, I've felt attacked! When acting out of what I believed to be a pure heart, I've found my motives questioned.

Oh, I've always had people in my life who have inspired me to believe in myself and convinced me that my cause was just and my course straight— thank God for those relationships. But the pressures of battle have amplified the voices that antagonize my efforts, doubt my faith, and slander my activities.

Sometimes the voices that fuel my loneliness are audible and alienating. Other times a lack of support leaves me feeling like I'm on an emotional and spiritual raft adrift, alone, in the sea of uncertainty. But no matter the source, the expression, or its intensity, it is always uncomfortable.

One such demonstration of devil-inspired tactics to get me to back away from my goal of serving God with an authentic faith, bold convictions, and humble service came as one of my closest friends pointed out some imperfections I was working hard to overcome.

At the request of my youth pastor, I was sharing a devotional thought with my youth group while on a trip. I had not pridefully sought to bring a word of correction to my peers by focusing on an area that I had perfected. I was intentionally, but uncomfortably, highlighting something in my life I was continuing to struggle with. I was going to talk about loving others.

Because there were some people on this trip that my human nature wanted to reject, wound, or ignore, my selfish tendencies and a decided *lack of love* had been on display over the previous few days. As my opportunity to share approached, I was painfully aware of the times—even that day—that I had lived outside of my desire to be a testimony of God's grace, acceptance, and love.

With fear and trembling, I began by reading a Scripture and offering a simple prayer, asking God to make our time fruitful.

Seated on a stage in the unfamiliar church where we were staying, I was surrounded by many of those whom I had lost my temper with, hurt with words, or gossiped about. The eyes focused on me that day also included friends who had willingly participated with me in the art of slander, bitter sarcasm, and judgment.

The intimacy of the format didn't allow me to slip into the persona of "all-knowing-and-supremely-confident-presenter." Instead, the faces in the crowd peered into my soul, making me feel exposed. I knew I had to address them without mask or pretense and spoke with a sense of confession.

I shared for ten or fifteen minutes about this part of our calling, and, to be honest, it got easier as I continued. I sensed the Lord's pleasure at my willingness to expose my frailties and express my regrets. The accountability of open disclosure gave me hope that perhaps one day I would be able to overcome my selfish reactions and offer others the unconditional love and acceptance God had extended to me.

However, I did not finish on a high note. Trisha made sure of that.

A girl I used to date (and evidently had hurt), made strong eye contact as we were moving toward the end of our time together. Once she had my attention, with me in mid-sentence, she mouthed the words I despise—and they cut me like a knife. Although there was no volume in her statement, it tore into my heart, enflaming my insecurity and guilt, as Trisha declared, *"You are a hypocrite!"*

Ouch! I had laid myself bare, exposing my sins and wounds and laying out my emotions on the table, and instead of protecting me or speaking words of forgiveness, Trisha had poured salt on my wounds!

Needless to say, my talk came to a quick and whimpering close. My countenance dropped, my volume died out, and my conviction waned. Instead of finishing boldly with the need to let God teach us how to love others and support one another, I abruptly ended without the energy to lead the group in prayer.

The most difficult thing for me was not the pain that Trisha had inflicted upon me; it was the fact that I knew she was right—or at least I thought she was. I now understand that hypocrisy is different than weakness. I used to think that every imperfection revealed condemning hypocrisy. Now, I realize that my convictions and character are still a work-in-progress, and that even areas I've allowed God access into haven't experienced full restoration yet.

But in that moment, my heart agreed with Trisha. *"I am a hypocrite."* The accusation created a sense of aloneness in me that no young person should ever feel. There I sat, in a group of my own Christian peers, squirming and floundering inside like a fish out of water, unable to find support or encouragement.

Although I knew some people there would have likely offered kind words and emotional assistance, the only feelings I had at that moment as I swung there from my limb of vulnerability were guilt, shame, and complete isolation.

The disconnect between my desire to love and my ability to do so was something I had to face alone. The nagging sense that I would never be qualified to carry God's message to others was intensified by the reminder that I had not even figured out the most simple of his principles for myself. The tragic thing is that having no one to turn to for fear that they will be judged or ridiculed separates many would-be champions of the faith from the accountability and encouragement often required to move forward in God's plan.

I'm grateful to say, however, that in this instance, the story didn't end with Trisha's cutting words, but with the wise and affirming counsel of my youth pastor.

As I finished my talk, he obviously noticed the change in me. As soon as I was done, he had everyone gather with a partner to pray about the matter I had discussed. Proactively, he pulled me aside and told me he wanted to talk.

As I began to explain how Trisha's words had devastated me, he did not agree with the indictment. Instead, he saw some signs in me that encouraged him. He knew I wasn't perfect, but he also recognized that I wasn't hiding from God, but that I was openly asking Him to refine me and help me overcome my sarcasm, pride, and selfishness.

After five or ten minutes, my confidence began to return. Instead of dwelling on words that separated me from hope, I began to focus on those that inspired it. Rather than feel judged for past failures, I sensed anticipation in my youth pastor for what I was becoming, which inspired expectancy in me as well.

"Instead of dwelling on words that separated me from hope, I began to focus on those that inspired it."

Left alone, my courage disappeared, accusations resounded, and discouragement found a home. But when someone who believed in me stood beside me and broke through my loneliness, those symptoms reversed. In a short time, I returned from the desert of despair and became re-planted in the fertile soil of faith. I was back on the warrior way.

Although it would be nice if every person trying to live for God had the appropriate support, the truth is everyone who wants to live a radical lifestyle of surrender and make intentional choices to embrace purpose and pursue destiny will—sooner or later—experience the curse of loneliness.

Occasionally its attack will be fairly mild, other times painfully awkward, and still others, absolutely debilitating. But whatever the intensity, it must not be allowed to run its course. If not dealt with correctly, whether you call it loneliness, aloneness or isolation, it can wreck havoc on the life of a champion. Just ask Samson.

Maybe It Wasn't the Hair

I have a theory. I know Samson's strength was found in his hair—but do we attribute his struggles to its loss when perhaps the blame lies elsewhere? Now, I know that his poor choices in women definitely played a part, but could even that be credited to something other than moral weakness and hormonal stupidity? Could loneliness or isolation have played a role in the foolish decisions Samson made that ultimately destroyed him?

From a young age, Samson's desire to find companionship led him all over the countryside. He did not care who they were, what they stood for, or what he would be giving up in exchange for their friendship; he wanted to escape loneliness, and he would do anything to ensure this success. Searching for camaraderie, his convictions and standards were compromised.

Interestingly, the Bible does not mention any male friends in Samson's life. Apart from his parents and the three women that we will discuss briefly, his most heralded acquaintances were "friends for hire," purchased to help him celebrate his wedding. I can't help but wonder if history would have treated Samson more kindly if he had a Jonathan-and-David type of relationship in his life. Perhaps such a bond would have helped him overcome his moral weakness and kept him on the right path.

Whether he ever sought male friends or not, we can't really say. And, certainly, pride and arrogance played a role. However, I believe it was largely the desire to overcome the curse of loneliness that drove Samson to make hasty and morally bankrupt decisions with the fairer gender.

I like to think that Samson was unaware of how unreasonable he was being in his pursuit of a companion. It was only natural for him to look for a wife, but surely he knew of the Old Testament prohibition against marrying a non-Jew. In any case, while looking for someone to complete him, he constantly settled or sought for a woman whose only commendable qualities were visual—if not heathen.

Spotting the charming woman in Timnah, Samson was drawn in by her beauty before he took time to discover what she was like. His parents were concerned that she didn't share their faith in the Creator (whenever a warrior settles for someone of questionable faith, trouble is guaranteed), but because she would take away his aloneness, he discounted their comments and demanded to marry her.

> ## "If loneliness had not over taken him so completely, perhaps Samson would have had the patience to wait for a godly relationship."

Before their marriage ceremony ended, she chose her Philistine friends over Samson, manipulated him, cost him a bet, and was given to be another man's bride. The episode ended harshly. To repay the debt for the lost bet, Samson killed thirty men. And later, tied torches to the tails of foxes, turning them into arsonists that incinerated the fields of the Philistines. The Philistines then had his formerly-promised wife and her father put to death.

If loneliness had not over taken him so completely, perhaps Samson would have had the patience to wait for a godly relationship.

The second recorded installment of Samson's relationships is even more tawdry. The wrath of his enemies was increasing and their pursuit of him was intensifying. This elevated his sense of isolation. Feeling like you are constantly under attack and that no one is in the foxhole with you can easily amplify emotional needs. So Samson chose a prostitute.

Was he simply seeking the physical pleasure this one-nighter would ensure, or was he craving the closeness that comes with that? I believe it was Samson's desperate desire to alleviate his aloneness—to have someone listen to him, to understand him, just to be with him—that forced him into the arms of such an ungodly woman.

Not surprisingly, this episode also ended badly. Samson's mission to bring deliverance to God's people could have ended here again, as his loneliness drove him into another vulnerable place. When the Philistines discovered that he had gone into this "house of pleasure," they hid outside the gates waiting for the opportunity to ambush him. Sensing their trap, he rose in the middle of the night, uprooted the city gates, and carried them to the top of the hill facing the city. Evidently, this demonstration of strength scared off his attackers!

The third woman Samson had a relationship with is definitely the one he is remembered for (movies have been made). Rather than risk being alone again, he flirted with his life and destiny, and fell headlong for Delilah. When she asked how mere men could overpower him, three times he falsely answered his love; however, the fourth time, he released his secret.

As they say, "*Love is blind*"—let me add, "*and slow to learn.*" Even though the deceit in Delilah's heart is obvious to all who read of their affair, Samson was not willing to see the obvious. She was clearly more concerned with his capture and the financial gain it would bring to her than with Samson. However, he continued playing her deadly game. After she twice tried to have him captured, he told her that the source of his great strength was in his hair, telling her that if his locks were braided, he would lose strength.

After he woke from a nap to discover Delilah had betrayed him yet again, he still wouldn't admit the insincerity of her love. Finally, after her nagging continued (*"How can you say that you love me if you won't tell me your secret"),* he revealed the true source of his strength. *"If you cut my hair, I will become as any other man."* The rest is history. He awoke to discover that his head had been shaved, his strength had departed, his woman had used him, and the Philistines had captured him.

From our vantage point, it is easy to declare Samson an ignorant fool, but should we perhaps consider that he was willing to sacrifice his unique purpose and strength for a little companionship? Could it be that Samson thought he could hold onto Delilah if he became as other men? Perhaps by sharing the secret of his strength, the warrior was declaring that he would rather be an ordinary man with a companion than a revolutionary who would forever endure the curse of isolation?

Although it is easy to judge Samson's choices, I think his life is a picture of how some with high calling will respond when asked to choose between destiny mixed with loneliness and a mundane life of mediocrity where relationships are readily accessible.

It grieves me to admit that there are one-time warriors and should-be warriors in the world today that are not engaging the enemy. Some have sacrificed their uniqueness on the altar of companionship. Because standing out was too difficult and being alone too painful, some have ignored their convictions, lowered their standards, and embraced relationships that diminish their effectiveness as it pertains to Kingdom business.

"Some have sacrificed their uniqueness on the altar of companionship."

I would rather live on purpose and let God take care of my social and emotional needs, than forfeit my integrity and surrender my destiny.

Learning to Lean

Stepping out of normal levels of commitment and traditional systems of ministry has also thrust me into places where I have felt isolated and alone. Typically, the onslaught has not been verbal or aggressive, but subtle and unspoken.

The looks I received from peers at school when I reached out to someone unpopular convinced me that I was on my own. The whispers I heard about being "holier than thou" simply because I chose to bow my head and pray for a meal at lunch, or not receiving an invitation to some activities because of my convictions, all increased the loneliness I already felt because I was choosing to stand up for Christ and against the culture.

Unfortunately, many of those who acted against me were not the un-churched people I was around; non-Christians typically respected the strength of my convictions. No, the majority of the time it was members of the so-called "Christian community" who rolled their eyes, whispered behind my back, or tried to get me to conform to their comfort levels. Sadly, the greatest pressure to compromise my faith came from Christian friends!

Unfortunately, this dynamic did not disappear as I matured and my circle changed. In obedience to the gentle nudges of the Holy Spirit, I chose to pioneer a new path of ministry in 1995. This new direction did not fit into the typical or traditional pattern of the local church. Rather, it was a para-church ministry established to come alongside local churches and partner with them to reach the students of their community.

As you can imagine, this direction infused me with energy as it captured so well the desires of my heart and the designs for which I believed God had created me. However, to my dismay, few people were excited for me. For reasons that I still can't explain, people close to me began to criticize my plans, saying that I was walking in arrogance and trying to *"make a name for myself."*

Once again, the thing that cut the most about these comments was their source. They were coming from people very close to me—people whom I had served beside in ministry. Those who used to trust my discernment began to accuse me of having prideful motives and selfish dreams.

I simply couldn't understand how Christian friends could turn on me so quickly.

Of course, the condemning barbs hurt. In a season when I was venturing out into unknown territory where doubts and questions were abundant, I learned that I couldn't even rely on the people closest to me. Loneliness haunted me. Self-doubts hounded me. For a season, I was discouraged.

However, it was during that trial that I learned one of the most important lessons in my life. I discovered that when humanity rejects you and leaves you to scale the mountain alone, God is still with you. In those moments, if you will look to Him, He will sustain you, encourage you, and help you climb toward your calling.

> "I discovered that when humanity rejects you and leaves you to scale the mountain alone, God is still with you."

I have often wondered what my trek would have looked like had I not been kicked out of the comfortable nest of some of my relationships. I can't help but think the journey would have been more fun and the climb more brisk; however, I also might not have learned to rely on my Encourager the way that I have.

Warriors will confront loneliness. Feelings of isolation and rejection will torment people with aggressive faith and strong callings. However, it's in those lonely places that the on-purpose Christian will prove God's faithfulness and friendship.

It's in the dry, "desert" times, where champions of the faith learn to lean the hardest on Him.

Chapter Six

Loneliness: A Warrior's Curse

Thought For The Day:

God desires to invade the shadows of your loneliness
with light that brings comfort, hope and courage.

Scripture Theme:

Psalm 23:4 "Even though I walk through the valley
of the shadow of death, I will fear no evil, for you are with
me; your rod and your staff, they comfort me."

Questions To Ponder:

Do you take other people's words
to heart more than God's?

Have you ever sacrificed your uniqueness
in order to feel accepted?

How can you defeat the loneliness that is bom-
barding your morality? Are you willing to be
alone temporarily if it is what God asks of you?

Digging Deeper:

Judges 14–16 records Samson's relational
mistakes. Check it out, it's an interesting read.

CHAPTER 7

Perseverance: Blaze Of Glory

There comes a time in every battle when the adrenaline-enhanced energy is gone and weariness sets in. Sometimes it comes after setbacks or defeat. Other times, the sense of fatigue follows extended struggles that have lasted longer than expected.

Every wise warrior knows that at some point he will hit a wall where disillusionment and discouragement await, yet its reality continues to catch many off guard when it comes into view. If the trial hits him unexpectedly or with greater ferocity than anticipated, he could give up his dream and slip back into mediocrity.

The ability to push past the struggles and challenges is key in every battle. Only those that will themselves toward patient endurance will taste victory. Discovering optimistic perseverance is key for all who want to affect their culture and influence history.

"The ability to push past the struggles and challenges is key in every battle."

This principle is valid and visible not only in spiritual warfare and kingdom pursuits, but in sports as well. On many occasions, I had to push past the desire to quit prematurely in order to achieve my goals. Such was the case in my epic (in my mind) battles with Steve Newhouse.

Before Steve and I ever stepped onto the basketball court together, he was my sworn enemy (a fact I never shared with him). He had all of the accolades and skills that I wanted. A small college All-American his junior year, he played my position and could shoot lights out. I looked forward to our first meeting.

His senior year was my first. I knew of him, but I was sure he had not heard about me. I wanted that to change. I vowed that I would stop him. Defensively, he would be my responsibility. Offensively, I wanted to play up to my potential.

The week leading up to the game against Steve's team, I worked especially hard. I watched extra film, ran extra sprints, and spent time visualizing the game. In my pictures, I did not give Steve any open shots, and he could not stay in front of me. My team won every imagined contest.

The morning of the big game, I woke with a ton of energy. I could not wait. As my team took the court, I looked toward the other goal to discover that Steve looked shorter than I had anticipated. Not only that, but he had a bulky brace on his right leg that stretched from his mid-thigh to his calf. His movements looked almost arthritic. Surely this could not be the great Steve Newhouse. I was unimpressed.

But, as the game started, the stud I had heard about and watched on video showed me that he was for real and my visualizations had been a lie. With great ease, he scored thirty-eight points that night leading his team to a resounding victory over mine.

It got so bad at one point that my coach removed me from guarding him choosing instead to try another defender.

As the game ended, I was humiliated. I had such high hopes, and they all crashed and burned in my home gym. I snuck home ashamed and embarrassed. I did not talk to anyone but slid into my bed trying to make sense of what had just happened.

The next day I went to practice and had to relive the entire episode as we dissected the game tape. With each ankle-breaking crossover that left me in the dust, I felt the glare of my coach. Every drained jumper moved me toward despair.

As we took the floor to practice, my coach called me aside and told me that Steve was a tough cover, but I was going to have to do a better job next time around if I wanted to guard him. As the words, *"next time"* left his mouth, I perked up. I remembered that since Steve was in our league, I was going to see him again. Each year we had a home-and-home series with divisional opponents, and at the end of the season we would visit their gym. I knew what had to be done. I had five weeks to prepare to meet him again, and I was going to be ready.

For a split second I realized that if I wanted to, I could have opted out of covering him. The coach would have allowed me to switch defensive assignments letting me guard another less-talented player, but I did not want to take the easy way out. I wanted to guard Steve. I wanted to prove to him that the first game was a fluke and that I could hang with him.

The week of game #2 arrived, and I was feeling good about the work I had put in. I had improved dramatically in past weeks, and I had been playing well. But that did not stop the memory of my failure against Steve from visiting.

History said that I would not be able to control his drives, stop his shot, or get past his defense. My collapse against him was still fresh in my mind, and my recent success against lesser talent had not diminished that fact.

As I lay in bed the morning of the game, there was a battle going on: my will to win versus the questions about my ability to do so. My competitive nature that rarely backs down was being aggressively confronted by the thought that if I gave away the assignment of guarding the All-American, I could save face.

But, right there, I made a decision. I was determined to give it my all and not back down until the final tick had expired from the game clock. Honestly, I was not sure how successful I could be, but I was resolved to let Steve know I was on the same court as him.

Willing myself to carry an air of confidence, I got on the bus for the two-hour ride, looking for the coach. Sitting down with him, I boldly declared, "*I want to guard Steve.*"

"When he realized I was determined to accept the task, he knew I could be trusted."

Checking my eyes for confirmation, he replied, *"OK, he is yours."* That is all the conversation that we had. When he realized I was determined to accept the task, he knew I could be trusted.

As the ball went into the air for the tip, I was ready, and when the ball swung back to me fifteen seconds into our first possession, I calmly buried a three-pointer. It was on.

On defense, I worked harder than I ever had in the past. I did not take one play off. I did not leave him to double-team or drift to stop cutters. Steve was my sole focus. Anticipating his drive, I stayed in front of him, and sensing when he wanted to launch his shot, I got a hand up. That night, Steve had to work for everything. And, by the end of the game, he knew he had been in a war.

My team lost the game (we were not very good), but we felt good about keeping it competitive. The first time out, we lost by twenty-plus, the second time, only by seven.

The game that night was not about two teams. I will forever remember it for the personal battle that I had with the senior who had all of the awards. He did score nineteen points (one of his lowest totals of the year), but he committed five turnovers and shot a poor percentage. On top of that, I almost matched him. I scored sixteen points on five fewer shots.

As we walked off the court, Steve gave me that *"it's OK to be a jock and hug another guy"* embrace. In that moment, I knew I had gained his unspoken respect. But that was not the only appreciation I received that night. As I walked into the locker room dripping with perspiration and exhausted (I had worked hard), my coach came over and congratulated me. *"Sean, you did a great job out there tonight. I am proud of you."*

With that, my one-sided rivalry with Steve Newhouse ended. And, although I would have loved the opportunity to meet up with him three years later when I had more experience and his arthritic knees had stiffened, I took great satisfaction in the fact that I did not give up.

The first time we met, I was embarrassed. However, I worked hard and got another shot. I persevered through the personal trial and came back to prove that I could play with him. I was content with my attitude and effort. My rival respected me. And my coach was proud. What more could I ask for (oh yeah, except the win)?

Finding Courage after Failure

Samson was bald, blind, and in prison. His head had been shaved, and mercilessly, his eyes had been gouged out. As he sat in the dank dungeon, he rehearsed his life. He remembered exploits of uncommon strength. He recalled the sense of energy that flooded his body as he killed the lion with his bare hands and ambushed thirty men to collect their clothes. With a smile on his face, he remembered gathering the 300 foxes, which he used to release 150 frantic live torches into the fields of his enemies. He thought of the time he destroyed 1,000 trained soldiers with only the jawbone of a donkey as his weapon.

As he thought about his battles, he had no remorse for all of the lives viciously killed. However, questions still haunted him. Had his siege against the Philistines been short-circuited because his relationship with Delilah stole his focus? Had his God-given purpose been achieved?

Never did a man bring him low. Actually, every man who stood in his path cowered as he came near. But Delilah had been his undoing. Her warm smile, fragrant aroma, sweet words, and gentle touch had led him to this blind existence where he might never again sense the thrilling presence and power of Almighty God using him to combat unjust oppression.

Although he was disappointed by the decisions and poor resolve that brought him to this uncomfortable dungeon, he took time to think about who he was and what he wanted. As he listened in the silence, he heard the gentle movements of God. He wasn't alone in that cell. God was right there with him, and as soon as he realized it, he began to shift his focus. Rather than concentrate on the failures that dominated the landscape of his life, he began to enjoy the company of the Creator.

Although he had lived his life as a violent ambassador for Israel and God's purposes, he had never taken time to get to know the Leader. In the heart of the jail, he had plenty of time, and since there was no one else to steal his focus, he started to listen to God and learn from him. He basked in the glow of his glory and began to enjoy his tender whispers.

His obsessive need to combat loneliness should have been intensified in this prison of isolation but the opposite occurred. God began to meet those needs. Aware that God was right next to him, Samson's seclusion proved to alleviate his aloneness.

For weeks Samson was hidden away. The great warrior, brought low. The mighty man, who had destroyed many, was humbled. His enemies assumed that his spirit was being broken with each day that passed, but the opposite was actually true. When tossed into his humble hole, he was consumed with regret and haunted by failure, but as he overcame loneliness and established his connection with God, he was not being broken—he was being built.

As his hair began to grow back, so did his passion. The courage and confidence that used to rule his life began to return. The righteous fury was beginning to burn once again. He was not sure if he would ever be used to restore order and punish the enemies of God, but his desire to do so was intact.

God has a habit of providing second chances to wounded warriors who have been put on the shelf, and he did for Samson as well. The inflated egos of the Philistine leaders decided to celebrate the capture of the notorious revolutionary, so they threw a party with Samson as the guest of honor. Intending to make a spectacle of their enemy, they brought him into the temple. Their desire to mock the strong man proved to be their undoing.

> **"God has a habit of providing second chances to wounded warriors who have been put on the shelf, and he did for Samson as well."**

The blind Samson requested that his attendant lead him to the columns in order that he may lean against them. However, once there, the might of the warrior reunited with the spirit that had already returned. Asking God to use him once again, he pushed with all of God's might and the temple came down. Because the Philistines and their leaders had gathered in drunkenness to watch the display, the temple was packed. As the columns imploded, the balcony fell killing both the people that stood on it as well as burying alive those underneath.

That day Samson experienced the greatest victory in his impressive history. His life was sacrificed along with his enemies, but going out in a blaze of glory was better than he could have ever hoped.

The foundation for that moment was crafted deep inside the dungeon as he sat all alone with God day after day. When he confessed his frailties, God forgave. When he expressed his regrets, hope began to stir that God would provide another chance for him to demonstrate his courage.

It would have been easier for his unique and brave spirit to die in that dormant place, but the warrior inside chose to remain alive. His circumstances were drastically hopeless, but he continued to look for his opportunity, and when it presented itself, he was ready. He did not allow his failures to destroy his dream. And he did not go out without a fight.

"He did not allow his failures to destroy his dream."

Not Giving Up

In my life, I have discovered that my greatest successes immediately followed my greatest failures. I am not talking about minor mess-ups—but catastrophic, devastating, and confidence-shaking fiascos. In the middle of such disappointment, I have questioned my ability to hear God, live for him, or do anything of significance. On more than one occasion, I have considered giving up on something before I saw it through. But as I summoned the courage to stay the course, discouragement turned to excitement. Emotional and spiritual success followed. And God proved faithful.

One incident (I could list many through the years) came in the beginnings of my ministry to youth. My first official job as a youth pastor came in San Jose, California. As a young man, nineteen years of age, I took the position convinced that I had the energy, personality, creativity, and passion to be a great youth pastor.

With an arrogance that would make my elders cringe, I jumped into the task of building the youth group's attendance. But, after two years, it had not grown. We began with six and ended with four.

The last several months of my stay there, I questioned everything about myself. *"Perhaps I am not called to this. Maybe someone else could do it better."* The lack of success sapped me of strength.

Emotionally, I was as low as I had ever been. After all, I had focused on becoming a youth minister since I was fourteen. Now, I was discovering that I might have made a mistake. The uncertainty hovered around me and the doubts became deafening.

About that time, I received a phone call from a pastor in Colorado. He had heard about me from a mutual friend and was calling to see if I would be interested in helping him build a healthy youth ministry in his church. It did not take me long to sense that this door was of God; however, before I wholeheartedly embraced this new challenge, I had a conversation with God that went something like this, *"God, I will go to Colorado, but this is it. If I don't see success at this church, I am done with ministry. I will get a retail job somewhere before I will put myself through another miserable experience."*

Although I did not tell the interested pastor about my reservations, the ultimatum that I had given God was direct and sincere. If Colorado proved to be another failure, I was going to quit. With limited expectations, I headed toward Colorado ready to give youth ministry one last try.

By that time I had been stripped of the pride surrounding me. I knew that my personality was not enough. My charisma and energy were tools, but they could not carry me to success. I arrived with a keen awareness that I needed God, or this was going to be a waste of everyone's time.

The first Wednesday night that I met with my new students, we had seven. But something supernatural took place. The numbers began to grow. Students were coming who had never been to the church (or any church) before, and God was touching them.

Within two months we had grown to over eighty. After four, we were over 120. In the first six months of our ministry, we had to move rooms three times because we kept outgrowing them.

But it was not just an increase in numbers. God was being God. Every week non-Christians were giving their lives to Christ. Prodigals were running home to their heavenly Father. And struggling Christians were discovering the courage to stay in the fight.

My *"last attempt at youth ministry"* ended up being one of the greatest experiences of my faith and life. If I had listened to the voice trying to convince me to throw in the towel, I would have never discovered the richness of ministry that I did those years in Colorado. To be honest, I am not sure what I would be doing now if I had quit, but I do know that I would not be walking in my calling; I would be searching for joy and significance, and many of the lives that have been touched as a result of God's faithfulness through me may still be searching for meaning and value.

My experience, as well as that of Samson, brings to mind a verse that encourages us to not quit. *"Let us not become weary in doing good, for at the proper time we will reap a harvest if we do not give up "* (Galatians 6:9).

Packed with truth, this Scripture reminds us that even though we despair, grow tired, and wonder why the fruit of our efforts is not greater, we cannot quit. For around the next corner—in a very short time, we will see the results of our labor.

Warriors know that they have to persevere. Every defeat brings them closer to victory; every failure, closer to success.

Chapter Seven

Perseverance: Blaze Of Glory

Thought For The Day:

> Great victories are just around the corner.

Scripture Theme:

> James 1:2-4 "Consider it pure joy my brothers, whenever you
> face trials of many kinds, because you know that the testing of your
> faith develops perseverance. Perseverance must finish its work so
> that you may be mature and complete, not lacking anything."

Questions To Ponder:

> Are you letting your past experiences
> discourage you or mold you?
>
> When you want to quit something do you
> trust God enough to follow his lead?
>
> How can you let God use your defeat for his victory?

Digging Deeper:

> Read Judges 16:23-31 to read the story
> of Samson's greatest victory.

CHAPTER 8

Insecurity: A Paralyzing Force

The internal antagonist taunts. With whispers of frailty and rehearsed failures, the most subversive of foes lays siege to potential world changers and history makers. Its name—Insecurity! Its goal—Paralyzation.

Although most attacks warriors face come from without, insecurity's assault comes from within. This enemy of potential turns the focus from the cause that is demanding a response to the weaknesses that limit, inferiority that holds captive, and the angst that declares the battle will end in defeat.

Instead of a visible opponent that points its finger showering its rival with verbal venom, the voice of insecurity gently whispers in the voice of the one being accused. Intimidation spouts, *"You can't...you won't...you didn't."* Insecurity is more difficult to detect and defeat since its approach is, *"I can't...I shouldn't...I am dreaming."*

The internal voice that mocks in the language of *"I"* is masked in a blanket of indisputable logic that steals hope and defeats the will. If the will is defeated, victory is improbable. Undeniable gifts can be rendered useless if insecurity keeps the would-be warrior from entering the battle.

"The internal voice that mocks in the language of "I" is masked in a blanket of indisputable logic that steals hope and defeats the will."

Israel's history revealed such a conflict. Literally head and shoulders above every other man in Israel (he was a full head taller), Saul was still struggling to discover confidence. Everyone else saw a leader worth following, a warrior in the making, and a potentially great king; yet, his inner voice convinced him that he was a wannabe. Even when Samuel told him he was God's choice to be the first king of their nation, the bleeding insecurity that shrouded him was not satisfied.

Timidity spoke internally. *"I can't do this. Who am I kidding? I don't know how to be king. I can't lead. I have nothing to offer these people."* Finally, the climax of the argument surfaced. *"God must have made a mistake. Surely he didn't mean to choose me."* As those voices were embraced, Saul found himself hiding...in the luggage.

The entire nation had gathered to applaud the chosen king, but he was nowhere to be found. With God ready to promote, anoint, and empower, he slipped out of sight hoping that his absence would allow time to reconsider the candidates. However, God knew what Saul could be.

Representing God and ready to act on his choice, Samuel called for Saul. When he did not emerge from the crowd, the Lord told him that he was hiding among the baggage. There, cowering in the corner was the one who had been handpicked to be Israel's first king; the one mighty and valiant men were waiting to follow.

When he was finally standing in front of the persistent prophet and kingmaker, he felt exposed. Although the people were overtly impressed and ready to fall in behind their new leader, the called-out warrior was not ready to lead. He was stuck between the internal voices in the language of *"I"* and the external voices that spoke of promise, anointing, and gifting. He wanted to believe the voice of Samuel, but the whispers of insecurity were louder.

Perhaps there was a moment in time when Saul secretly told Samuel that he had picked the wrong person, but Samuel would not buy it. He knew that the Lord had chosen Saul. He knew that God would give him the ability to do what he had been called to do—if he was obedient. He knew that the striking man standing before him was fashioned to lead a nation; he just needed some courage.

Saul had every gift needed. He was equipped with intellect, strategies, the leadership necessary, and the ability—but he didn't have the confidence. That would come. But first, Samuel needed to pour the oil. He needed to give him the authority. He needed for Saul to understand that God never asks you to do things that he will not help you do.

In God, everything needed is offered, and everything missing is given. Every weakness is balanced, and every strength is made stronger. When God calls, he equips. When he puts people in challenging situations, he does so knowing that they can succeed if they trust him. But they will only thrive if they listen to the voice of the Encourager instead of the internal negative voice that speaks in the language of "*I.*"

"In God, everything needed is offered, and everything missing is given."

Sometimes I Need Encouragement

Looking back, I can recall several instances in my life where the lying whispers of insecurity worked to convince me to give up after a strong start or even before I attempted to move forward. One such story took place in a gym where I worked while I was in college.

As an extra source of income, I was opening a health club in San Jose, California, five days a week. Although I was around free weights, weight machines, racquetball courts, and pools, I never took advantage of them. To be honest, I hated lifting weights (I rarely did it), avoided doing anything aerobic unless there was a basketball involved, and I did not watch my diet at all (greasy burgers and huge cokes were a daily routine). You never would have known it before my metabolism slowed down in my mid-twenties, but I was woefully out of shape.

Therefore, when the guys working in the club began to pressure me to compete in the mini-triathlon, I resisted—not because I was afraid to lose or because I was afraid of the work—I refused to compete because I knew that my need to contend at a high level would outweigh my poor conditioning. To put it simply, I knew that if I joined, I would push myself too hard and I would regret it later.

The event consisted of three indoor events, which did not sound difficult but I knew myself. If I signed up, I would go as hard as I could, which would be much harder that I should. I would pick a pace far above my ability or conditioning and I would hurt because of it.

Well, my co-workers (personal trainers who had big muscles and bigger egos) continued pestering me to join even though I kept saying, "*No.*" I was politely declining their offer to compete, but they began to play dirty—they began to talk trash. Gary said, "*Sean, are you afraid that you will be embarrassed? It's OK; no one expects you to do well, but you should at least try.*"

Something inside of me goes ballistic when that kind of gauntlet is thrown. I ignore all logic, come out of my little shell, and respond in kind. "*Gary, the real reason I don't want to sign up is because I am not in shape. And when I go out and beat all of you gym rats who work out hours every day, I will feel good, you will feel bad, and when I get home, my body will regret that I pushed it so hard.*"

As you can imagine, Gary jumped on my comment, and the game was on. So on Saturday I showed up for my first of three timed meets. I would be racing against a clock, and the results would be posted on the board for everyone in the club to see.

The first competition was the treadmill. Although I had played around on this apparatus before, I had never seriously run for any distance or time, but I figured I would push it as best as I could.

They placed the machine at a 3% incline and started the timer for the five minutes allowed. Because five didn't seem like a lot, I figured that I would increase the speed until I couldn't stand it any longer. By the time I had picked my aggressive pace, I was clopping along at a good rate.

Toward the end of the five minutes, I was getting very tired. I reached up to lower the speed, but Ken wouldn't let me. He was the official timer for the triathlon, and he was in my face telling me how great I was doing. *"You can't slow down now; you are on a record pace."* I tried to reason with him and tell him I couldn't do it, but he still wouldn't let me slow down. With obnoxious volume and tone, he was encouraging me for doing well and reprimanding me for wanting to quit.

Finally, the five minutes ended. The machine was turned off. I placed my hands on my knees and searched for breath but found none. It seemed as if all oxygen was strategically avoiding me. My lungs were burning. My heart was pounding, and my mouth was dry. I was in physical pain.

In that moment, I heard the internal voice. *"I can't do this. I am not in shape. There is no way that I can keep this up. I had better quit now before I really hurt myself."* As I listened to the voice, it began to make sense. I looked up at Ken and told him that I was going to quit. But he would have none of it. *"Sean, you can't quit; you did great. You did better than great! You killed Gary on that."*

He had not convinced me that the reward was worth this level of sacrifice, but I was finding my determination again. His voice of strength was over-powering the internal voice of struggle. So without much conscious thought, I found myself on the Aero-dyne bike ready for the second event.

The Aerodyne is a contraption different from a regular bike in that you use both your arms and your legs. Your legs work as if it were a regular bike, but the arms pump handlebars that create force as well. In the middle of the bars there is a needle that tells you how vigorously you are cranking away.

When Ken told me that I could begin (we only had one minute breaks in-between events), I kicked it hard. My arms and legs were churning away, and the needle was jumping. When it reached the 7, I decided to hold steady.

That is when Ken looked over my shoulder and said, *"Sean, if you can hold that 7, you are going to do well. I think Gary only held a 6."*

Those were all the words that I needed to hear. With newfound motivation, I kept up my pace—for one minute. Sixty seconds into my Aerodyne expe-rience, my exerted energy mixed with my lack of training was reminding me that I was in pain. My lungs were screaming, as was my heart. My arms, legs, back, and even my head were aching with considerable volume.

I turned to Ken, *"That's it, I need to quit. I can't do this. I am not in this kind of shape. Everything about me hurts."*

But he wouldn't let me. *"You can't quit. You are doing great. Keep going. I am not going to let you wimp out. You need to show Gary. Come on..."* Directly in front of my face, he loudly declared that I needed to stay in the game.

Although I didn't want to, and the internal voices tried to convince me that I would die if I continued, I made it the next four minutes until I could stop.

Getting off the bike, I went directly to the fountain. If I could not fill my lungs and slow the pace of my heart, at least I would be able to ease the dryness in my mouth...or so I thought. Turns out, I was breathing so intensely that my mouth was not working correctly. My lips could not lap water. My tongue could not bring it in.

"That's it. I can't do this. My body is shutting down. I have to quit. There is no way that I can beat Gary. What am I thinking?" But when I expressed these things to Ken, he wouldn't even listen. He just helped me get onto the third piece of equipment and got the clock running.

Another piece of machinery that I had never used, this particular rowing machine was used to train college-level rowers. I know this because one of the guys that worked at the club used to row on such a team. As I just said, I had never touched this rowing machine, but I had seen it run violently. I had watched this former rower work out, and I knew that a good day for him was keeping the needle pointing directly toward the ceiling. So after I got started and my initial push tripped the vertical point, I set that as my goal—to keep the needle pointed straight up for the entire five minutes.

Just as on the Aerodyne, my vigorous start was difficult to sustain. Thirty seconds in, I was beginning to feel it. My legs grew weary and my back ached. My arms wanted to turn to noodles, and my inner organs were still struggling with the pace of exertion.

The thoughts returned. *"I can't keep this up. I have to quit. I may be doing permanent damage to my body. If I don't walk away right now, they are going to have to carry me home."*

When I began to express my inner turmoil to Ken in a whiny *"please let me quit, I am exhausted"* voice, he wasn't hearing me. *"There is no way that you are quitting this close to the end. Come on, keep it up. You are doing great. You can't quit. You are on fire."*

"When I began to express my inner turmoil to Ken in a whiny 'please let me quit, I am exhausted' voice, he wasn't hearing me."

Well, the distraction of Ken's encouragement made the time pass by more quickly. Before I knew it, the five minutes was over, and I was off the rower laying down trying to catch my breath.

Although I went home sick that afternoon, I was glad that I did not give up. I was thrilled that I had finished. Oh, I did not come back for my two other time trials—after my body revolted against me for close to a week for pushing myself so hard, no trophy was worth putting myself through that again; however, I was authentically pleased that I had finished.

And, I had done well. Turns out that even though I had not trained, my body argued with me the entire way, and I had only used one of my three opportunities to post my best time, I placed in the top five out of over two hundred competitors—I actually beat Gary.

But I would not have done it if I had not listened to the slightly obnoxious but tremendously encouraging voice urging me on. If "*I can't*" would have won out over "*Oh, yes you can,*" I would have started strong but never finished. I would have missed out on the opportunity to feel good about my accomplishment, and I would not have had the chance to remind Gary that a skinny guy with a strong competitive nature is a force to be reckoned with.

"If 'I can't' would have won out over 'Oh, yes you can,' I would have started strong but never finished."

In the same way, I have discovered that life is filled with opportunities to settle for mediocrity. As our inner voice tries to alter reality in the language of "*I,*" it steals hope and poisons the will. Its tone is convincing—so convincing that it is easy to accept its opinions as reality.

If we listen to that voice, we may actually begin to believe that we don't have what it takes to overcome a sin in our life. That perhaps God did make a mistake when he called us to take a leadership role. Or, that we are wasting our time trying since there is no way that we can succeed. If we listen to that voice, we will either refuse the assignment or we will not finish, no matter how strong we started.

However, if we listen to the spiritual voices that are birthed in what will be if we trust, we begin to push toward God's best for our lives. We keep fighting the sins that are working to dominate us because the voice of "*I AM*" declares that he will teach us to overcome. We continue to pray great prayers because he says that our requests are powerful and effective. And we stay focused on our dreams because we know that the heavenly voice tells us we have a destiny.

Like prizefighters in the ring, the two voices slug it out trying to gain an advantage in the lives of the warrior. Whichever one is embraced will win, and whichever one wins will be the star in the script of the warrior's life.

Chapter Eight

Insecurity: A Paralyzing Force

Thought For The Day:

> If the will is defeated, victory is impossible.

Scripture Theme:

> Philippians 4:13 "I can do everything
> through him who gives me strength."

Questions To Ponder:

> What voices are louder in your life:
> Insecurity or Encouragement?
>
> What is one thing you can do to drown
> out the voices of Insecurity & Doubt?
>
> Who encourages you in your walk with
> God? How can you encourage others?

Digging Deeper:

> To read of Saul's royal appointment
> read Isaiah chapters 8-10.

CHAPTER 9

Impartation:
Recruiting For The Revolution

When I arrived at the college I had chosen to prepare for ministry (actually, I had chosen it for other reasons: i.e., the beach was close, the weather was appealing, the girls on the brochure were spectacular, and the sports program was solid), there were two things I loved: basketball and myself.

As a Christian who had dedicated his life to serve God vocationally I would have said in a heartbeat that I loved God. But looking back, I'm not sure I did.

I loved the culture—the feeling—that Christianity provided me. And I loved the, um "social opportunities." Believe it or not, I loved the guidelines I had adopted for my life. And, of course, I certainly loved the benefits and blessings of being one of God's kids. (I was thrilled about that heaven versus hell for eternity thing.) However, I'm not sure I loved God.

My faith was all about performance and my Christian life about impressing people. And sadly, it was about the accolades that came as I self-righteously lived the rules better than most of my peers. Like a contestant in a strong man competition, I flexed my spiritual muscle while sporting a holy tan and a pious smile. I know, sick but true.

"My faith was all about performance and my Christian life about impressing people."

Don't get me wrong. I wanted my faith to be real. I simply did not know how to make it so. That's when I met Rob—a warrior. He found me, called me out, and inspired in me real faith.

Because I was a certified basketball fanatic, the two-hour practices on my college team didn't satisfy my need to pursue my obsession. So I became the proverbial "gym rat" and found myself spending lonely hours on the hardwood before and after our organized sessions. Since I never tired of the game, I was forced to shoot, dribble, and play imaginary games in isolation. (Hey, don't laugh. If you've played the game, you've done it, too.)

One day while shooting free throws, another student walked onto the court and asked if he could shoot around. A couple inches shorter than me, but visibly stronger, Rob proved to be a good companion as he came in a close second at being the most zealous basketball fan on our campus.

Although I was eighteen and Rob was twenty-eight, Rob and I became instant friends. I discovered that he had enrolled in college after spending several years in the Navy. Before too long, Rob and I were meeting on the basketball court three times a week after my practices were over and playing marathon games of one-on-one. Not to the typical scores of fifteen or twenty-one, but to 150…by ones. For hours we would battle back and forth competitively, aggressively; both determined to win at all costs. When our games were over, we would walk up the hill from the gym with smiles on our faces and sweat pouring off of our bodies.

When Rob looked at me, he saw something more than a point guard. In fact, I'm convinced he also saw beyond my faith façade. He recognized someone with a calling, but poor priorities. He saw past the shiny exterior and realized I didn't know how to connect with Christ. Though I never shared with him my questions and personal frustrations, Rob must have known I was searching for something a bit more real in my faith. And, for some reason, he decided he was going to invest time in me off the court. He wasn't interested in telling me how to live my life, but showing me how he lived his. And not so I'd become more like him…so I'd learn what it meant to be more like Jesus.

During one of our walks up the hill, Rob asked me if I prayed. Almost offended that the sincerity or practice of my faith would be questioned, I quickly responded with a, *"Yes, of course I pray."*

He asked, *"What does your prayer life look like?"*

The confusion that rose in my heart as the question sunk in must have been visible in my expression. I didn't know what to say, so I stumbled around, searching for something to hide my embarrassment. Interrupting my stuttering attempt, Rob said, *"Tell you what. I will pick you up tomorrow morning at 5:30. We will go pray together."*

My first thought was about the time. I wanted to shout, *"Are you kidding? 5:30?"* But I knew that would expose my lack of desire and discipline, so I bit my tongue. I couldn't think of a good excuse. (Except for sleep, my schedule seemed clear at 5:30 A.M.) I told him I'd be up and ready.

After setting my alarm for 5:15, I climbed in bed, and tried to drift off to sleep. It was then I began to think about our meeting, and I realized that I was in trouble. I feared that my shallow faith—and ignorance in prayer—was going to be a sad display. My insecurity and apprehension stole sleep, but eventually, I drifted off.

When Rob quietly knocked on my door that morning, I was ready, albeit foggy. We walked to his car, got in, and drove to a summit overlooking the surf. With the car still running, we rolled down the windows, and Rob put in a worship tape. We began to pray.

"His prayers weren't memorized, rehearsed, or even dry. They seemed real, relevant, and inspired."

He began to pray out loud. Shocked and uncomfortable, I began to pray under my breath.

As I listened to Rob, I was amazed. I had never seen anyone (his age, at least) talk to God like he actually knew Him. Whereas I felt as if I was reading my prayer list from some religious page in the newspaper, he was connecting with the Creator of the universe. He actually seemed to be responding to what he later would inform me were the "*prompt-*

ings of the Spirit." His prayers weren't memorized, rehearsed, or even dry. They seemed real, relevant, and inspired.

We sat there for an hour (which was more than enough since I had reached the end of my list and prayed for everything I knew to pray for after about seven minutes) before he looked at me and asked to pray for me. There in the car, he took my hand and began to pray that God would become real in my life. Even this prayer wasn't the religious-type of prayer I was used to. It seemed to come from a sincere part of his heart. I could sense he knew something that he wanted me to know, and he was simply asking God to reveal to me this amazing discovery that had defined his life.

After the prayer, I sat speechless all the way back to the dorms. Although I still coveted my sleep, our meeting became a habit. Three times a week, we would begin the day by driving to the beach before most on campus were awake.

After just a short time, I started to feel like I was finally connecting with God. The vertical relationship that I sensed in Rob's life was intriguing to me. I wanted what he had. And, the more time I spent around him, I began to understand I already had it—I began to identify how to draw close to God, hear the *"promptings"* that I had heard about. I also began to sense God's pleasure whenever I would come before Him.

Over that semester, I observed many things as I closely watched Rob. It was the first time I had ever seen anyone worship God privately. Never before had I witnessed anyone weep as they began to express the love and grace of God he felt in his life. I also saw someone whom I respected ignore his reputation in order to live by conviction and be an authentic witness of faith. I saw in Rob a role model of attractive Christianity.

While considering all of the warriors whom I have known, I realized I'd be remiss to leave Rob off the list. The way he lived his life—the intensity of his faith…made him my hero.

I don't know how much our prayer times impacted me in areas of courage, hope, honor, and godliness (it's impossible to compare who you are with who you could have been if circumstances had been different), but I'm grateful I don't have to. I'm sure that Rob would not want to take credit for all he did for me (he would be sure to direct all thanks and appreciation towards God), but his intimate connection with Christ and his adventurous approach to living life boldly helped me transition from a dull and boring life of religious behavior to an exciting and fascinating relationship with my Creator.

Looking back, I recognize in Rob one of the defining qualities of Jesus Christ, the ultimate warrior, and our role model. They both were recruiters.

Jesus realized that his character, passion, and perspectives must be passed on, for without duplication, his impact would be limited. Rob chose me, Jesus chose twelve. Bona fide warriors will follow their example and invest in others.

With a forward focus, warriors understand that recruiting and training the next group of men and women with courageous faith is imperative. They work to identify those with promise and offer resources, experience, wisdom, and encouragement in order to make them successful in the battles that lie ahead.

Jonathan, one of King Saul's sons, understood this principle very well. Although it would have been easier to engage the enemy on his own, he invited along an apprentice. Not because he was looking to borrow bravery or he needed companionship, but because Israel was short on soldiers with faith. The young prince recognized an opportunity to inspire a future leader.

At the time, the climate in Israel was all too familiar. Philistines ruled the land. They were unavoidable, their power insurmountable. They were like locusts in the land. Their domination of the Israelites was complete. The control they exhibited reached beyond military personnel and stretched to activities that touched common people and routine activities.

Hope was gone. Desolation, despair, and despondency were evident. Israel was in disarray. The soldiers who had stayed to fight the antagonist had slowly slipped away in fear until only 600 men remained with Saul. But even those men were not equipped to make war as only two swords remained in all of Israel. King Saul had one, and young prince Jonathan had another.

Although a small remnant with warrior's desire remained, their actions were apprehensive. They gathered together waiting. They hid in fear. God was not satisfied with the static approach and the apprehensive posture. So, he went looking for a warrior… and he found one in Jonathan.

The enemy of the land was not as real to him as the God he served. Fear did not have a stronghold on his life because faith had captured him. He had an indomitable spirit.

Sitting under a tree one day, inspiration hit him. Devotion rushed to the surface. He knew that he must do something. The conditions of his people were demanding action.

With conviction simmering in his heart, he knew that something must be done. The numbers were not in his favor, but courage spoke, *"Nothing can hinder God by moving, whether by many or by few"* (I Samuel 14:6). Convinced that a great victory was only an aggressive and faith-filled stroke away, he determined in his heart to move out and engage the enemy.

Satisfied that God was on his side and the inspiration for his campaign was from above, he knew that something amazing was about to take place. *"For the Lord and for King Saul"* could have been his only cry, but he saw another opportunity. He was not looking for a companion to strengthen his valor; he was looking to share his life and the impending victory. He was going to deposit into the faith of one younger— less experienced.

With a glimpse toward his young aide, he remembered that the greatest way to pass on faith is to invite someone on a remarkable journey and allow a victory that can only originate in heaven to brand the heart. *"Hey, I am about to go do something that sounds crazy. Would you like to come? God has been speaking to me about coming out of hiding and going to war. God is on our side and there is no way that we can lose. You up for a battle? You want to take a chance with me?"* (I Samuel 14:6).

Without hesitation, his armor bearer said, *"Let's go."*

The reckless response and willingness to follow Jonathan came from admiration. An intense desire to be used for the miraculous raised him to his feet. When the invitation came he willingly jumped at the chance, ignoring the danger. As he followed his guide toward their rival, his heart was pounding with expectation. He could not wait to see what would happen.

"An intense desire to be used for the miraculous raised him to his feet."

Intense, yet expectant silence accompanied them until they were standing below a cliff where the Philistines were camped. To the men at the outpost, the threat of two isolated soldiers seemed insignificant—almost humorous. They began to mock the revolutionaries, calling them up the crag and promising to feed their bodies to the birds of the air.

Confidence brimming, Jonathan climbed to the top with his aide behind. Irreverent men dressed for battle ran to him, but they could not get through his defenses. One by one, they fell.

Wanting to maximize the faith of the armor bearer, Jonathan did not kill them. Instead, he encouraged the one behind him to complete the task. More than twenty lost their lives that day as a direct result of Jonathan rejecting complacency and defying the regime of the day.

As the skirmish intensified, it spilled over onto Saul's army. Seeing the activity and realizing that something divine was transpiring, the rest of the army joined in the fight, pushing the Philistines out of the territory and restoring order to the land.

After hours in battle, a tired Jonathan and an exhausted armor bearer joined the rest of the troops knowing that the multi-faceted victory had truly been inspired. Jonathan's actions had begun an insurrection and stimulated an entire army. The Philistines were on their way out and the Israelites were on their way back up.

A quiet moment followed Jonathan's violent day. As he looked across the fire at his aide who was sharing with some of his young friends about their activities, he recognized faith in his eyes and confidence in his posture. He heard tones of loyalty in his speech, loyalty both to himself and to His God. Jonathan saw bits of himself coming out in his friend.

Gazing through the smoke that rose from the burning logs, he silently prayed that the heart of his young friend would be forever changed by the activities of the day. *"Lord, deposit into his life, the heart of a warrior. May he be willing to fight for you and your purposes from this moment on. May he never be afraid of his enemies, but inspired by faith, angry at injustice, and established in love for You. May he aggressively go to war whenever and wherever you need him."*

Intentional Investment

Every relationship is an opportunity to share our convictions and beliefs. So, why is it that we usually build walls to keep our faith in and others out? Rather than see opportunities to offer faith, we avoid the faithless. Instead of strengthening the weak, we treat them as diseased.

The warrior way is this: Instead of hiding from those different or less mature, warriors engage them. They offer hope and faith that is expressed authentically. But they don't do this through a stale sermon; it's revealed in every day life. Occasionally, it will be inconvenient—uncomfortable even, but as the Holy Spirit leads, God will open up exciting doors and you will see fresh breath enter into those who are lifeless.

"We need to always be on the lookout for others whom we can invite to higher plains of principle and purpose."

The old saying, *"the more the merrier"* is only true on certain occasions and in particular circumstances. One of those times when it should become a motto to live by is in battle. Like Jonathan, we must pray to have an indomitable spirit, be Spirit-influenced, and rarely try to go it alone. We need to always be on the lookout for others whom we can invite to higher plains of principle and purpose.

When we see in someone potential with limited faith, the best way to help them is not to talk with them about faith, but let them see ours. When our eye falls on a person who doesn't have passion, ours must rub off on them. And if we recognize a lack of discipline, let's get around them and offer them what we have.

Impartation is a goal of true Kingdom warriors. Training the next generation in order to proclaim the truth and advance the cause is a worthy pursuit.

Moses invested in Joshua and he became a great leader. Elijah invited Elisha to join him in life and the second prophet's accomplishment doubled the first's, building on the foundation left. As mentioned earlier, even Jesus trained twelve to share His faith and carry on His work. If it was that important for them, don't you think it should be a priority for us?

Is there someone who needs what you have in order to be all that they can be? Perhaps there is a potential warrior waiting for you to notice them and show them how to love God, battle the enemy, and live aggressively.

Chapter Nine

Impartation: Recruiting For The Revolution

Thought For The Day:

> It is appointed unto a man once to
> die, but his legacy can live on.

Scripture Theme:

> II Timothy 2:2 "And the things you have heard
> me say in presence of many witnesses entrust to reliable
> men who will also be qualified to teach others."

Questions To Ponder:

> Are you influencing those around you
> in a positive, life-changing way?
>
> Are you aware of the power you
> have to influence others?
>
> What are you going to do to influ-
> ence those around you for Christ?

Digging Deeper:

> The record of the attack by Jonathan
> is found in I Samuel 14:1–14.

CHAPTER 10

Intimidation:
The Unwanted Companion

Intimidation desires to be a factor in all of our lives. And it doesn't whisper so much as yells. That's the nature of intimidation. It's not trying to stealthily come through the back door, but it barges right into your face.

If you're an athlete, then you know that intimidation on the field of play is obvious. A loudmouth taunt and an obvious stare can make an opponent think twice about trying to play their best, and about coming into occupied territory.

In competition, it's predictable. In your walk of faith, it's a bit more hidden. But because of its persistence it is a serious threat to our faith, our convictions, and our spiritual dreams. Why? It comes from a dark enemy.

Whether you've been a Christian a short time, or whether you're a long-termer like me, you need to be aware that whenever you try to muster the courage to pursue a God-given goal using the gifts He's given you, you'll be confronted with the taunts of the intimidator. For me it's been a constant back and forth battle to find trust, hope, and belief in the midst of a sandstorm of insecurity, failure, and opposition.

It was a Sunday evening when I received a phone call at home. My wife Mary and I were playing a game with some friends after eating dinner. I was told that a young man I had known named Carl had died the night before. He had taken his own life.

As I drove out to a lonely cemetery on Wednesday to watch them lower this young man into the ground, I reminisced. I remembered the first time that he had come to our youth group with friends from his school. He was kind and soft spoken, respectful and friendly. His originality showed through in his style. He always wore dark clothing with a heavy overcoat. He gave the impression that he flirted with the grunge movement, but was unsure if he wanted to fully commit.

I got to know him conversationally over the next several months, though we did not have any deep or serious talks. I didn't know much about his family, his dreams, his fears, or his passions. I was not aware of his past or his upbringing. I knew only the generic details of his life, and things that I had picked up and discerned in a hurried and barely-there relationship.

Although I'm certain he had heard of the unconditional love of Jesus Christ and the way to begin a faith relationship in the ten to fifteen times that he had attended, I could not be sure if he had ever surrendered his life to Christ.

Arriving in Elizabeth, Colo., I turned right onto the driveway that led to the graveyard. The sight took me back a little. There were hundreds of high school students who had come out to bury their friend. Getting out of my car and walking toward the casket, I began to observe the teenagers who were present. I watched them as they hugged and cried. I watched some walk off by themselves, consumed by despair. Others gathered in circles of three and five to talk in whispers.

Standing there in the midst of all that pain and depression, I tried to sort through my feelings and impressions. I wanted answers to questions that were swirling in my mind, but was not allowed much time for introspection. The grief of Carl's friends grabbed my attention and would not let go. Looking into their eyes, I saw hopelessness. The same type of hopelessness that Carl must have felt the day he took his own life. I sensed indescribable pain and paralyzing heartache. I saw in the eyes of many an overwhelming desperation.

Although the setting amplified their misery, I was caught off guard as I recognized heartache and anguish that was not new to these young lives. Their pain had not been birthed the moment they heard Carl had taken his life. The events of that day only served to intensify those feelings.

"Oddly, I felt as if I was the one under attack."

I stood there in stunned silence. But it wasn't the silence that comes from an absence of talking. It was an absence of God's light and hope. It was a spirit of intimidation. Oddly, I felt as if I was the one under attack. My heartbeat was irregular, my breathing labored. I tried to look away, but couldn't. My focus rested on student after struggling student. They wrestled not only with the loss of a comrade, but with life itself.

And then I sensed the whispers. *"You are losing. They are mine. No matter how hard you try, you will not win.…You can not win."*

Trash talk doesn't have to come from a burly linebacker. The devil was aggressively trying to convince me that my passion to share the love of God with students would only end in despair. He was trying to shake my confidence and erode my faith that God was going to ultimately win the battle for the soul—and eternity—of this generation of young people.

> ## "And staring back at me through the windshield were the images of the empty eyes of hurting students: the stare of intimidation."

Forty-five minutes later I was back in my car driving home. A depressive hopelessness continued to ride shotgun. And staring back at me through the windshield were the images of the empty eyes of hurting students: the stare of intimidation.

Like any normal follower, I don't win *every* battle of intimidation. At various times in the past, I have been bullied into inactivity, scared silent, and ultimately rendered ineffective. Even my desire to pray has been encroached upon.

Although smugly silent or brashly sarcastic in their expression, I have heard contemptuous shouts from the culture telling me that my faith is irrelevant. And then the expected chorus of angry and uninformed jeers from the media who are trying to prove that all Christians (especially ministers) are insincere and hypocritical. I have seen disdain in the gaze of those who have not found faith as I have openly shared my love for Christ in truth and conviction. This opposition has convinced me that although tolerance is encouraged, the rules often change when it comes to Christianity.

"It's in these times that I realize that if I don't conquer intimidation... intimidation will conquer me."

I have even felt the personal onslaught of aggressive anger come at me in articulate expression trying to convince me that my mission to share the love of Christ is invasive and unwanted. One such email read, *"What can I do to get your manipulative, insincere spots off of my radio station you blasphemous, hypocritical freak."* It's in these times that I realize that if I don't conquer intimidation…intimidation will conquer me.

I remember back to a Bible story from my youth. One among those so familiar that it bordered on irrelevancy. At least until I start connecting the dots between my cemetery experience and this biblical story I've heard so often.

David and Goliath suddenly no longer becomes a kid's story but a lifeline to solve the intimidation factor I face. You remember the story, don't you?

Boldly the Israelites gathered in a corporate expression of aggression. Clothed with armor and equipped with swords and shields they formed the ranks away from the camp, on the top of the hill, gazing into the valley. Hoping to work themselves into a righteous frenzy where someone was willing to take action, they screamed at the top of their lungs, shaking their iron blades above them.

But did these *"mighty warriors of God"* ever get beyond the war cry? Nope. They never even entered the battle. Gazing at the enemy below, intimidation became their unwanted companion and terror became the thief that stole their hope.

What Saul and the other Israelites saw as they looked towards the valley made something inside of them snap. They were not full of faith and hope. They lost sight of the cause. They were afraid. A trash-talking giant was making a mockery of their army…and their God.

Even the mighty King Saul was intimidated. He became incapacitated, worse…debilitated. All who stood and watched the giant march into the valley were defeated men. They never lifted a sword in defense of their God and people. There was not an ounce of courage among the entire army. And…there was not a mustard seed of faith.

Their emotions were dominating their thoughts and stealing all confidence. Intimidation was winning before the battle had even begun. Their hearts were beating hard and fast. Not with excitement, anticipation, and adrenaline, but with fear, anxiety, and woe. I can imagine that their mouths were so dry that they could not even encourage each other. Their breathing was laborsome. And their postures were slumped over, weary from a battle that they refused to enter, a fight they were convinced could not be won.

The downward spiral of inactivity, fear, and confusion invited chaos and embraced insecurity. And that is when the taunts began to rise up from within. No longer was Goliath the one mocking; their own inner voices began to disrespect these men of war. *"No courage! No honor! No warriors here."*

Although they had tried to shout themselves into frenzy and discover courage in a corporate expression of aggressive confidence, when the mask was pulled back and the truth was told, these men had been exposed. They didn't know how to trust. They were void of hope. Faith was absent. Coward was their name. Although their intentions were good, when intimidation entered the scene fear gripped their hearts and they never got beyond the war cry.

Like this picture of cowering men, intimidation in my life has usually been instigated by an external force: a person who stands in opposition or a circumstance that looks hopeless. Pointing a terrorizing finger in my face, logic overcomes faith so that my courage remains silent and invisible. If I don't deal with the derision early, the threats and taunts from others soon become my own voice trying to talk me out of the battle that lies ahead.

I have discovered that I am my biggest critic and my most persistent foe. I am the one who rehearses my past mistakes and dwells on my recent failures. The loudest and most painful attacks on my character, abilities, desires and fortitude come from within. If I don't recognize that attitude in my heart, that negative thought, then it begins to simmer.

"I have discovered that I am my biggest critic and my most persistent foe."

In the ever-changing landscape of my life, I have discovered a few things that never change: God is always good, sin is always destructive, faith is sometimes confusing, and…intimidators are always active.

There is always a battle raging around me, in me, and for me. Good fights against evil, and evil against good. Confidence is confronted by insecurity and faith by doubt. What I want to be and have decided that I will live for is attacked, challenged, and put to the test.

I've learned that intimidation is an unwanted guest hiding in the shadows and waiting for us all. Its desire to dominate true believers is strong. However, with God's help, we can overcome. We can step up, unafraid…just as David did.

The morning of the funeral I had prayed that God would call a generation to Himself. Driving away it seemed like an empty dream: a distant hope. But ten minutes into that homeward journey, something happened in my heart.

I ignored the intimidating glare of hurting students and began to gaze toward heaven. And then I stopped focusing on the whispers of the intimidator and started to focus on the unchangeable truth and security of God's Word. Then I dug deeper. I remembered God's loving heart and dying passion for those students. He hurts when they hurt. He longs to bring comfort and peace. He alone gives purpose and meaning.

In my car that day, hope won…and intimidation lost. The lies whispered in the cemetery did not take root in the way they were intended. Instead, they took my passion for those students to deeper levels.

As you are faced with the intimidating taunts from the voices of darkness, will you remember that Goliaths fall when the weapons of faith are used to sling them to the ground? Will you recoil into obscurity when the trash talk gets too loud?

Or will you choose the warrior's way?

Chapter Ten Summary

Intimidation: The Unwanted Companion

Thought For The Day:

When God is on your side there is no reason to fear.

Scripture Theme:

> I John 4:4 "The man who says, "I know him," but does not do
> what he commands is a liar, and the truth is not in him."

Questions To Ponder:

Do you let the enemy speak intimidation into your life?

Are you hiding in your tent of insecurity,
or are you fighting the good fight?

Are there things you know God has asked you to
do but you have been too intimidated to try?

Digging Deeper:

I Samuel 17 is a historically accurate account
of Israel's refusal to fight Goliath.

CHAPTER 11

Perspective:
The Warrior's Outlook

The first day of fall practice my senior year it was understood that I would be the starting quarterback on the first day of the season. Not, however, because I had earned the position. I was inheriting it by default.

After three years of not playing football, I was recruited to fill a void. Ken, the official starter, was suspended for disciplinary action. The second-string guy had broken his arm during the summer and was not available, and third in line stood only 5'6". Because I had played the position in the past, some friends verbally manipulated me until I agreed to try out.

I went out for the team reluctantly, but as we began to practice, I started to enjoy it. On top of that, I was playing well. During practice I was making good throws and quick decisions. Much to the anguish of Ken and his friends, there were certain members of the team that believed I had a chance to supplant Ken as "*the guy.*"

Although Ken and I were as different as two athletes can be, we had similar goals. He was the avid partier and ladies' man, while I was the straight-laced Christian that every girl thought was a "*sweet, big-brother type*"; yet, there we were, both fighting for the same position, and surprisingly, for the same girl.

Tensions mounted as summer ended and the school year began. On a couple of occasions, Ken intentionally brushed up against me, either warning me to stay out of his way or trying to provoke me to do something that would give him an excuse to fight.

As practices continued to roll along I was staying right with the "stud quarterback." As the coaches affirmed me with positive feedback and complemented my play, Ken's resentment grew. It culminated at the all-squad scrimmage as I led my team to a strong showing and the victory.

With the girl on my arm (the girl voted best looking of our class had chosen me) and an immense amount of confidence, I went into the first game, ready to conquer the world and unseat Ken as the school's darling, coach's favorite, and the boy that could do no wrong. I was going to steal some of his thunder and make some noise myself. With a good showing, I was going to once-and-for-all prove myself.

The first series of the game was uneventful: five or six plays, a couple of first downs, then a punt. I came over to the sidelines not deflated, but slightly disappointed. My dream of scoring on every possession was gone, but I was not discouraged. That didn't happen until the second series.

The first play of the second series, I received the painful impact of a collision with an aggressive linebacker. Pulling myself off of the ground, the bruise that was left on my right hip reminded me about the injury that had forced me to leave football as a freshman.

Up to that point, I had not noticed the size or heard the smack talk of the other team, but as I neared the line for the next play, my view had changed. Instead of concentrating on my responsibilities, I glanced into the faces of the other team. Twenty-two eyes looking right at me like hungry dogs staring down steaks that they are about to devour.

The pace of my heart changed from controlled to chaotic. That is when my football career careened off the proverbial cliff.

As I dropped back for a simple screen pass, I did not wait for the play to set up. I rushed it when I sensed pressure. The pass came out slightly high and just a tad strong. Instead of falling to the ground incomplete, it bounced off of the running back's shoulder pad and into the air where it was located and intercepted by a defender.

As he grabbed the pass, something grabbed my throat. I had begun a cycle of perpetual choking that lasted the entire game. From that moment on, I did not do one thing right the rest of the day. Before the game was over, I had thrown four interceptions and fumbled twice. With my face mask in his hand, the coach verbally assaulted my mistakes; I sensed his relief that Ken would be back the following week.

I didn't play much from that point on. My competitive nature that has always been a driving and defining force utterly disappeared. I was satisfied not playing—actually happy that I was being overlooked.

Week after week as I stood along the sidelines, it seemed as if I was looking at all-star athletes that were inhumanly fast, strong, and gifted. Their abilities reinforced the insecurities that I was feeling about mine. My perceptions convinced me that I did not belong in the game; not an ounce of courage was left.

I was a member of my team in title and by uniform only. To an outsider, it may have seemed as if I was a team player who was putting in the practice and rooting in the shadows, but truth be told, I was only thinking about how I could avoid the frustration and embarrassment that I felt that first night of the season. I was hiding on the sideline hoping not be exposed.

Looking back, I am no longer embarrassed that I had a horrible night, but I wish that I could go back and ensure that the first game would not ruin my entire season. I have learned a lot since that fall night. One of the primary lessons is that focus is important. What we see when we look towards the conflict will determine the outcome. If faith speaks…we win. If fear…we lose.

When preparing to take a snap against 1,000 pounds of lineman, or trying to take a stand when friends tempt my actions, or swimming upstream against the culture's current, I have discovered that what my eyes communicate to my heart will determine what risks I am willing to take and what battles I am willing to enter.

On more than one occasion, unfortunately, when lenses of fear and confusion have convinced me that circumstances are hard, the devil is mean, things are hopeless, society is callous, and resistance is meaningless, I have backed down instead of stepped up. My perception sparked timidity and wound up destroying the confidence in the Lord that I normally have.

"I those moments, I sensed the stuff of warriors running through my veins."

But, when I have seen through eyes of faith, things did no look so bad. Courage declared that every problem had a solution; God was better than the devil was bad, every mountain was an opportunity to marvel, and I knew that the opposition would fall. In those moments, I sensed the stuff of warriors running through my veins.

Without a doubt, what you see determines your direction. A young David lived this principle.

It was not David's arrogance that forced him off the side of the mountain and into the field with Goliath; it was what he saw. Looking into the valley, King Saul and the army saw an enemy (big and undefeatable); David saw a cause (imperative and impossible to ignore). The army ran from what they saw. He ran to it.

For forty days, a giant named Goliath had arrogantly challenged anyone willing, to a personal battle. The result of their match was to determine the fate of both armies. Although seasoned soldiers heard the taunts of the enemy, no one mustered the courage to even consider the challenge.

Dressed in bronze scale armor, the giant also wore a helmet, which amplified his prodigious height (he was over 9 feet tall). Day by day, the foe played mental games with the militia standing on the rim of the gorge. His condescending taunts exploded through the valley leaving all his enemies scurrying for cover.

Everyone in the Israelite army was "dismayed and terrified." Paralyzed would likely be a better description. All hope was gone. Fortitude had disappeared, and conviction had vanished. Eighty times the would-be-warriors tried to muster valor, but eighty times they ran in fear. Their patriotism went missing in the face of the intimidator. No one was willing to confront the enemy. No one marched into the valley. No one shouted back. That is, until David arrived.

Plucked from his usual job of watching the sheep, sent to deliver food to his brothers and bring word of progress to his father, David arrived at camp as an unsuspecting bystander. He was unaware that the military heroes were refusing to fight, and that his countrymen were void of hope and saturated in terror. He expected to meet up with aggressive warriors; instead, he was greeted by passive soldiers who were intimidated by the enemy and introspectively posturing themselves for protection.

Thinking that the battle was about to be waged, David ran to the front to find his brothers and watch the action. As he stood on the brink of the hill, he saw Goliath for the first time. What began as a multitude of men dwindled, until one stood alone. Everyone withdrew quickly...except David.

"What began as a multitude of men dwindled, until one stood alone."

As if the weight of the words became blurry to everyone around, but piercingly clear to him, the scene shifted from a military operation of many to an isolated challenge that only David could hear and understand.

David's eyes locked on the enemy, but he was not intimidated by his size or his haughty words. David became incensed. As if all movement around him ceased, and all time slowed down, his focus became clear. His blood began to boil as righteous indignation was exploding in his heart like an atomic reaction.

What he saw and heard called out to the warrior inside of him. He could not ignore Goliath, and he could not look away. Because he was consumed by the cause, he readied to face the Philistine.

Like the Israelite army, there have been times when I have been so intimidated that I was frozen in inactivity; however, like David, there are also times when I have gazed into a situation and been moved to take action.

Back to Football

I'd been gladly sitting on the bench for most of the season after that first game. But something changed the night that we visited the Colfax Bulldogs. Instead of seeing the size of the enemy and pondering my lack of skill, I saw an opportunity...I saw a cause.

My team had been flying through the early games of the season as if we had been playing the little league teams for which I had played years ago. We (I say "we" with slight sarcasm, since I was not playing) looked great racking up win after win. The games weren't even close.

The only game that we had lost all season had been the 1st one (I was constantly reminded that was the one that I started), and the prognosticators were assuming that we would sweep our league. But the Bulldogs tried to take a bite out of that plan.

Looking back, I am still not sure what happened. Perhaps we came in overconfident. Perhaps, under prepared. I do not know what happened; all I know is that by the second quarter there was a confused and unfamiliar feeling on our side of the field. We were losing.

As I sat on the cold bench that night, my competitive nature began to come back. Looking at the field of play, I was getting irritated that my team was getting pushed around and shut down. For the first time in weeks I began to focus on the game. Although I was not going to get on the field for any significant plays, I began to root my friends on. Before long, I was standing instead of sitting. I was verbally encouraging rather than silently sulking. I was interacting with my team.

Shortly, something miraculous took place. And, I had something to do with it.

After another short and unproductive series by our offensive team (Ken was not playing well at all), the punting team was called out. Because coaches look for non-playing players to fill out this somewhat insignificant squad, I happened to be on that team. My responsibilities entailed counting to make sure that we had eleven players on the field, and calling the generic snap count that sent the ball from the center to the punter. I was the *"Personal Punt Protector."*

The meaningless activities of that position had long since lulled me to sleep, but as I surveyed the field something different happened. Coming out of the huddle, I began to count my counterparts in their red and white jerseys. To my surprise, Rob Griffith, the guy out on the end, was all alone.

Rob was the outside receiver whose job it was to corral the person receiving the punt. However, there was not a defender on him. Something inside of me said, *"Call a fake punt."* But that voice was not nearly as loud as the one that reminded me of my failures. *"You can't pull this off. You are going to screw it up."*

I only had a couple of seconds to think about my situation, but it seemed much longer. Looking into the eyes of enemy, I realized that if I took the snap and tried to throw a pass, I would become the object of their aggression (the one guy coming off the right end looked mean and nasty). From the other team, my mind drifted to the comments of my coaches and teammates after every poor pass that I had thrown in that first game and in practice. On occasion, they used words. At other times, their looks, laughs, and rolled eyes worked with my insecurity to convince me that they didn't trust me. I felt I couldn't do anything right.

The realization that my team needed a boost pushed away those negative thoughts clouding my mind. As I once again glanced at the opposing team, I was not afraid; I knew what had to be done. Not taking into consideration the ramifications of my hasty choice, I decided to call the fake punt.

The signal is out there; my team should know that something special is about to occur. However, no one heard me. The center who was snapping the ball did not hear me. The line that should have provided some sort of blocking and protection did not hear me. Rob, the guy that I wanted to throw the pass to didn't even hear me. The only person that heard me was that big and nasty with the bulldog on his helmet.

Although the snap was not intended for me, I was not going to let the ball pass. I had to move out of position, but I reached out and snagged the ball. The rush was aggressive, I could feel the eyes of the opposition bearing down on me, but my focus was elsewhere. My eyes were glued on Rob, silently begging him to realize that he was not guarded, I had the ball in my hands, and I was waiting for him to look at me.

With my time running out, I could wait no longer. I loaded up and heaved the ball down the right sideline hoping, pleading...praying that it would be caught.

As soon as I released the ball, I got thrown to the ground. Because I could not see the action, I listened. The initial silence was amplified as if the stands had inhaled simultaneously, leaving the stadium void of even common movement. Replacing the silence were both sounds of exasperation and exultation. From my sideline, I heard cheers, from the other, groans.

When Rob did not hear the punt, he looked up just in time to see the projectile in flight. He reached out and caught it in stride. Although he did not score (he got tackled on the 2 yard line), that play changed the course of the game. We went on to win by twenty.

When my view changed, I knew that I could not ignore the opportunity. As the need became more visible than the opponent, I got in the game and helped my team. This equation has proven itself time and time again in my life. When my perception illuminates the cause, the opposition begins to fade and my faith takes action. But, when my focus is captivated by the challenge, I sit on the sideline hanging my head, refusing to move forward.

"When my view changed, I knew that I could not ignore the opportunity."

You and I both know that living for and obeying God is not an easy task. You will face opposition and you will face conflict. You will either experience the onslaught of the enemy standing in the way between you and your goals or you will discover distractions nipping at your heels trying to slow you down.

Whether the antagonist that you face is external or internal, aggressive or subtle, paralyzing or simply irritating, how you perceive it is very important. If you allow faith to speak and command fear to silence, like David did 2,800 years ago, you also will see a cause—one that you cannot ignore. But, if you let apprehension and anxiety convince you to "sit this one out," then you will experience frustration, confusion, and defeat.

Not only that, but you'll get used to the sidelines. It will be more comfortable and less dangerous. Yes, it's likely you won't fail as much.

But...

Make no mistake: you CAN do everything through Him who gives you strength (the warrior's mantra). But, if your perspective keeps you off the field, then you WILL do nothing.

The true warrior loathes the sidelines and is willing to risk it all on the field of play. He knows that you cannot succeed unless you try.

Chapter Eleven

Perspective: The Warrior's Outlook

Thought For The Day:

Inactivity ensures defeat.

Scripture Theme:

Romans 8:38-39 "For I am convinced that neither death nor life,
neither angels nor demons, neither the present nor the future, nor any powers,
neither height nor depth, nor anything else in all creation, will be able
to separate us from the love of God that is in Christ Jesus Our Lord."

Questions To Ponder:

Is there an area of your life that
needs a new perspective?

Do you run from adversity when
you should be facing it?

Does your perspective line up with God's perspective?

Digging Deeper:

The heralded story of David's confrontation
with Goliath is found in I Samuel 17.

CHAPTER 12

Unique: One of a Kind

When it comes to artistry, there is no one who compares to God. He placed the stars in the sky to light the heavens. He carved out the canyons and fashioned the mountains. Every kind of terrain was his idea—from mountains to valleys, rain forests to deserts. Creatively, he conjured up every animal in the earth, sea, and sky, and then brought them to life.

Everywhere you look, you can see the handiwork of the Creator. But nowhere in all of creation will you discover something or someone more calculated and exceptional than you and me.

His creative genius is on display in us. We are the result of his brilliant design…not just our physical forms and operating systems, but the complete package comprised of our desires, qualities, feelings, capabilities, and capacities.

"He put great thought into us and takes great delight in us."

We are not the result of an impulsive moment of invention formed with leftover parts and tossed-away pieces. He put great thought into us and takes great delight in us. We have been crafted intentionally and specifically for the calling of warrior that rests upon our life. There may be some more gifted with music than us…more educated…or even more spiritually acute, but there is no one who can fulfill the dreams that God has for us.

We are originals…one of a kind. We are not clones, duplicates, or carbon copies.

Yet sometimes we reject the rare qualities and uncommon traits that God strategically placed inside of us. When we run from our uniqueness, we will not see giants fall and battles won. If we strive to conform to some other personality or method of ministry, we will continue to live frustrated lives of undiscovered potential and untapped strength.

However, with help from the Spirit of God, we can discover and embrace this uniqueness—those things that make us special—those that give courage, strength, and the ability to live the radical warrior life.

Learning to Break Out

Discovering who I was created to be and becoming comfortable in my individuality is one of the life lessons I have struggled to learn. Although I knew the spiritual adages that proclaimed me to be unique: *"a man fearfully and wonderfully made in the image of the Almighty God,"* I sometimes struggled to find self-confidence.

I think my problems came from the fact that I was unimpressed with what I saw in the mirror. Not only were my physical features less than I desired, the mirror also reminded me that I did not have the personality that held everybody in stitches, the spiritual gifts that were visible and admired by others, nor the shocking physical gifts that made me stand out. I felt very normal…average, and that didn't sit well with me.

My feelings of being common and ordinary were enhanced by all of the people surrounding me that were swimming in special abilities and superior personalities.

First, there was my youth pastor—it is a both a blessing and a curse to have such a great man in your life. He was my spiritual hero. And I wanted to be just like him. The problem was, my shortcomings were illuminated by the aura of his polished bust that I had placed on my emotional mantel. Because of my frailties, failures, and "average-ness," I was convinced that achieving his level of faith and impact was a dead-end dream.

Another person whom I did not measure up to well was Mark: a friend a couple years older who seemed to have all the right answers. He could turn every conversation funny. His Bond-like confidence and charm made girls swoon, and he had the spiritual passion of a zealot—yet his faith seemed authentic and personal.

I subconsciously built a shrine for him that created in me both comfort (I truly appreciated his friendship) and anxiety (I felt I could never measure up). And I tried to imitate him, thinking that I could be a more successful me if I was more like him.

But out of all of the people who enhanced my ungodly recognition that I was plain, the worst one was my brother, Byron. Only 15 months older than me in age but decades beyond me in terms of perceived personality, spiritual giftedness, and social skills, the one closest to me growing up was the one who unknowingly tormented me daily.

Early on, it seemed that Byron was the one who inherited all the comedic traits—I, on the other hand, sensed people laughing *at* me...not *with* me. My attempts at humor ended with a quick-witted comment hitting the ground with an uncomfortable thud as if a cinder block had been dropped from several stories. He could carry a conversation with many people, while I seemed to struggle participating in one.

The girls all found him more attractive and I had a broken heart to prove it: two girlfriends of mine became former girlfriends out of hopes that freeing themselves from any relationship entanglements with me might create opportunities with him. (I sound pretty pathetic, don't I?)

Even on the talent end, he seemed to get it all. When it came to drama, he would be cast as the cut-up—that one role written simply to add spice and humor—the one person whom everyone left the production talking about and imitating.

I, unfortunately, was not so fortunate. Typically, I received the roles that brought down the energy levels: the hyper-spiritual guy who only opened his mouth to spout some proverb, or "guy #3," who is vital to the presentation only because he adds balance to the stage but does not do anything meaningful or memorable the entire evening.

I seemed to lose every comparison, so somewhere along the way; I figured that if I could not beat my brother, then I should copy him. So that is what I did. Without making it too obvious (I think I hid it well), I started to dress like him (this is awkwardly visible in our senior pictures, where I actually was photographed wearing the exact clothes that he had worn the year before), talk like him, and I tried to adopt his mannerisms. But it didn't work. I did not yet know who I was, but after a time, I knew that I was not good at being him.

David, also, had an opportunity to imitate a warrior that he respected and who had experienced success—but it took him less time than me to reject the pressure to conform.

"I must be me."

Don't you hate it when someone tries to curb your enthusiasm and put a damper on your faith? Someone tells you that you are too young, not experienced enough, or not knowledgeable enough to accomplish the task at hand. They point out the risk involved, the improbability of your dream, or the weaknesses that they are convinced will surely lead to your defeat.

But they forget one very important element... the key ingredient that gives you hope and ensures victory. They neglect the "God factor."

They forget that you were created and crafted to live an aggressive faith. They overlook the promises of God, which ensure your protection, provision, and that his presence will always be with you. They overlook your unique qualities that make you powerful in God. Oh, they see the glaring weaknesses that you have, but they fail to see the richness, rightness, and might of God that rests upon you and will operate through you.

"They forget that you were created and crafted to live an aggressive faith."

That is the part of the equation that Saul was missing as he tried to bring a reality check to the young shepherd. *"Son, don't you understand that Goliath is a mighty warrior? Compared to him, you are inexperienced and insignificant."* The tone was condescending, as if he was saying, *"I know that you have great intentions, but you are really outclassed here. Why don't you leave this fight to the seasoned soldiers?"*

But that was the problem. Those qualified were not willing. Therefore, it was up to David—the only one convinced that the battle was God's to win. Saul's pessimism did not deter David. This would not be David's first battle. He had never before fought a giant, but he had fought. He had tasted victory.

While watching his father's sheep, there were occasions when bears and lions had come for a taste, but with David on guard, all were safe. More than once, he heard the distressed bleating of a lamb under attack and ran to its aide. Even when the situation looked hopeless and one from the flock had been taken captive, he would not give up. With relentless passion for the injured animal, he would chase down the predator and get his attention. With no fear in his heart, he would strike the lion or bear until it released the lamb. And if (or should I say "when") the furious animal would turn on him, he would seize it by the hair, strike it, and kill it.

Wow! What a picture: a teenage boy fearless in the face of an angry lion, grabbing its mane and beating it to death. David knew that the Philistine would discover the same fate as those bears and lions.

As Saul looked into David's eyes, he recognized that he could not—he would not—be deterred. Once he realized that his "logic" would be ignored, he changed his strategy. He no longer tried to talk David out of the fight—he offered guidance. (Note: People who are too intimidated to fight will many times try to offer controls and counsel to the fearless.)

As if he was declaring that the only successful exploits in battle would be won using the same methods in the past, he offered David his armor. *"Well, if you are going to fight the giant, at least wear the right gear. This is how I have always fought, and if you are going to be successful, then you need to do it the same way I have always done it.*"

Thank goodness David realized that God had not created him to look like Saul or fight like him. It did not take him long in the king's bronze coat and helmet with that awkward sword attached to his side to realize it was not comfortable. He could barely walk. In a battle, he would have no chance.

He shrugged off the limitations that were placed upon him by the king and declared, "*This is not who I am.*" In effect, he was *saying, "I honor tradition but I am not bound by it. Saul, I appreciate your help. I understand that you are an experienced warrior and that you have had success in your armor with your sword. But I am not you. I cannot use the tactics that make you effective. I am unique, and I have to be true to who I know God made me to be.*"

Saul did not believe that David could win the battle without proper training and equipment, but to prevent him from walking into the valley would mean that he would have to take his place. So he watched David walk away wearing his normal clothing and carrying only his staff and shepherd's bag.

Before David approached the Philistine, he stopped by the stream bed to choose his weapons. He needed only stones to turn a sling into a deadly weapon. Once the five stones were tucked into his pouch, he moved into the heart of the valley where

Goliath's verbal venom was still lingering.

When he saw the unarmed (or so he thought) boy approaching, his taunts turned from arrogant shouts aimed at anyone in the opposing army to a specific target. *"Am I a dog that you would come at me with sticks? Come here and I'll give your body to the birds of the air and the beasts of the field."*

Someone without confidence might have trembled, but knowing that he had been created for this moment, with assurance, David proclaimed the source of his strength (*"I come against you in the name of the Lord Almighty"*) and the prophetic outcome of the ensuing skirmish (*"I'll strike you down and cut off your head. Today I will give the carcasses of the Philistine army to the birds of the air and the beasts of the earth, and the whole earth will know that there is a God in Israel."*).

"He was not shaken by what he saw nor was he moved by what he heard."

David's confidence was not unfounded. He sensed the Lord calling him to the battle, his fury at the one taunting, and his presence that would prevail. He was not shaken by what he saw nor was he moved by what he heard. As he readied to face Goliath, the one invisible had captivated him.

So he ran. Not *from* the foe…*to* him. One rock was all he needed to bring down the giant. With supernatural velocity and divine trajectory, it found Goliath vulnerable. He fell face down into the ground. Dead! He was dead before he hit the ground…but the task was not yet complete.

As David stood over the fallen foe, he glanced up toward the king and his army. He gazed at his brothers who were standing with shock and surprise on their faces. He knew that these inactive warriors needed to get back into the fight. His actions that day were not intended solely to defeat one man; they were meant to ignite a multitude.

So he borrowed Goliath's sword…used it to cut off his head…and held up his trophy for his countrymen to see.

With Goliath's head in view, one army groaned and ran. Another shouted and pursued. One man died in the valley, but many others would fall before the day was over. David had laid one to rest; the others would not be a direct result of his sling…but you can be sure that they were the outcome of his faith.

David would not have been effective if he had tried to be Saul. He would not have succeeded that day if he had tried to fit into the mold that all other soldiers were fashioned from. But as one young man stood with honor and confidence before both the condescending comments of his "friends" and the angry voice of his enemy, he led an offensive that began a revolution.

I Sensed His Pleasure

David realized that his methods could not duplicate another's, and even though I loved his story as a little boy, I missed that profound truth in his encounter with Saul.

For a season in my life, I searched for meaning…value…individuality, but strangely enough, I tried to discover how to stand above the crowd by conforming to it. I tried on different costumes but none seemed to suit me. I could not be my youth pastor. I was not a good Mark and I felt phony imitating my brother. These failures made me angry. But it was this turmoil in my heart that first led me to sense God's pleasure and embrace my uniqueness.

I still remember the one moment in time when the issue came to a head. It happened when I was traveling with 40 of my friends in our church bus. A trip that should have been exhilarating and refreshing was, up to that point, exhausting and frustrating…not because my friends abandoned me, the trip wasn't productive, or there were any looming problems. The first half of my trip was miserable because…Byron was on the trip and my insecurity had stowed away.

That particular summer, Byron had shaved his hair very short for comfort and convenience. Being that his hair was tight to the head and soft, he inherited a nickname. Everyone called him Kiwi (everyone except me—too endearing).

Shortly after leaving Spokane, Washington, to travel down to a youth convention in southern California, we realized that the trip was going to be long and hot. Without an air conditioner (aren't those mandatory now?), our bus ride left the port of adrenaline and energy and ran aground on the shores of monotonous and uncomfortable.

Since this was before the age of cell phones, IPODs, and personal DVD players, the technological services to keep a group of teens engaged for two weeks (many of those days being locked in that slow-moving bus) were not present. So we sat…and sat…and waited…and waited.

Occasionally, we would find something that would capture our attention and distract us from the heat for short periods of time, but essentially, we were counting the hours until we could stop for the next meal.

Sensing an opportunity, Byron put his gift of entertainment to work. He decided to step up…to become the center of attention…to alienate his brother (ok, I am sure he never even considered the impact this had on me, but in the moment, I felt as if his blessing was my curse, and he unknowingly was plunging a knife into my proverbial back).

As we neared the end of the first day's drive, Byron loudly proclaimed, *"Kiwi's fun hour starts in five minutes."* Although no one knew what to expect, everyone on that bus crammed into the back three seats with anticipation in their eyes because *"if Byron is going to entertain us, it must be good."*

That afternoon, my brother became the host of his very own variety show. For one hour he coaxed laughter and song out of my friends and even my youth leaders. Doing impersonations, quoting movies, and orchestrating hilarity, he arrested the attention of all the beleaguered travelers.

Kiwi's fun hour was a hit. And it became a ritual. For 14 days straight, he entertained the crew. And a few of those days, he angered me.

I said *"everyone"* scooted back to participate in the program, but that is not completely true. There were still two people who did not get involved: the bus driver and myself.

Of course, the driver had a great excuse as to why he did not move toward the back. I, on the other hand, did not. I told everyone that I was staying up front to keep the bus driver awake (bad things happen if the bus driver falls asleep); however, the truth was, I was mad.

As I glanced back at Byron "doing his thing," I was angry that I did not think of it first…that I did not have a cool nickname…that I was not the comedian. Comparing myself to what I saw made me disgruntled. It was hard for me to be happy about what made me unique because jealousy was whispering lies that highlighted a void in my personality.

For the first five or six days, I stewed in my attitude of inferiority. Parts of me loathed Byron because of his gifts, while other parts loathed myself for being so ordinary.

I do not think I ever turned my disappointment toward God and began to blame him for making me average and awkward, but I certainly was not searching for those unique features that were gifts from him.

While returning to the church where we were staying after a great time at a Southern Californian amusement park (I got my picture taken with Minnie), Byron was in his place on the bus and I was in mine. Sitting near the bus driver, I was floating between the memories of the day and the personal torment that I was putting myself through. Emotionally, I was unstable. Shortly after enjoying rides, getting photos taken with cartoon characters, and drinking in the beautiful coastal weather, my attitude tried to slip back into discouragement.

My bi-polar nature was, for the first time, obvious to me (I am sure that others around me picked up on this long before I did). I recognized that the joy of my day was being stolen by my internal conflict. I had never seen it so clearly before, but I realized that I was being held hostage by my insecurity.

Frustrated at the unevenness of my feelings, I prayed. I asked the Lord to show me the source of my confusion and irritation. In that moment, I realized that I was not content with who I was—I had lived under that curse all my life, but until that moment, I had not recognized it.

Instead of dwelling on all of the things that I wished I was (my habit when *Kiwi's fun hour* was roaring through the bus), the Lord began to show me all of the unique things that made me special. I thought about the strength of my friendships—I had people in my life that I knew I could count on, and they knew they could count on me.

I was reminded that my youth pastor had been giving me opportunities to teach in different settings because he recognized the Lord's calling upon my life. Although I was still trying to discover confidence as I learned to share the message in my heart, I was encouraged that God had been promoting me even at a young age.

And lastly, I sensed God begin to gladden my spirit. Although I could not articulate the actual words, I felt his smile and his pleasure. As if the switch had just been turned on, I knew that if God had written me a letter that day, he would have declared that he was proud of me; and all of the talents, perspectives, passions, and abilities that I would need to fulfill God's good plan for my life had been intentionally placed inside.

I know it sounds too simple, but I can honestly tell you that from that day on, something in me changed. There were still times when petty jealousies crept into my life and encouraged me to covet something I saw in someone else I respected; but overall, God has been building in me strong confidence in the fact that he knew what he was doing when he made me.

And I am not ordinary. He made me unique. I am one of a kind. His calling upon my life is distinctly mine. I have been intentionally designed to accomplish the plan scripted for me. It is the creative brilliance of God that made me different than Byron and every other person on the face of the earth.

It sounds strange as it comes out, but I am the only me that God ever made…that now brings me joy instead of discouragement. When I look in the mirror, I now see a willing warrior—not one trying to fit into another man's armor (personality or ministry), but one who is learning to be content with the qualities and talents that have been assigned specifically to him.

I hope that you see the same when you glance into your mirror.

Chapter Twelve

Unique: One of a Kind

Thought For The Day:

There is a reason that there is no one else like you! As you walk with Christ you will discover what that reason is.

Scripture Theme:

Psalm 139:13–16 "For you created my inmost being; you knit me together in my mothers womb. I praise you because I am fearfully and wonderfully made; your works are wonderful I know that full well. My frame was not hidden from you when I was made in the secret place. When I was woven together in the depths of the earth, your eyes saw my unformed body. All the days ordained for me were written in your book before one of them came to be."

Questions To Ponder:

Are you realizing the potential of your unique personality or are you dwelling in the gifts of others that you may lack?

Do you know who you are as well as you know your closest friends?

Digging Deeper:

David Defeated Goliath using his honed ability in I Samuel 17.

CHAPTER 13

Opposition: Unexpected Attacks

Saul liked him—maybe even loved him...so why was he trying to kill him?

It wasn't that long ago that he was offering the young shepherd his very own royal armor to wear as protection...what had changed? Why was he now trying to pin him to the wall with his spear?

As he ran from the palace, David was confused. Fear had not gripped his heart. After all, this was not the first time that he had faced a foe that wanted him dead. He was, however, mystified...bewildered that a former friend—one that he longed to serve (as a good son assists his loving father)—was the one hurling the weapon. Saul, David's former mentor and a once strong advocate, was pursuing him.

After running a safe distance, the weight of the burning questions slowed him until he was pacing back and forth under a broom tree.

"What have I done wrong?" he questioned himself. *"Why does the King want me dead?"*

Although an adequate answer—one that painted Saul's behavior as reasoned and rational—never came. He did not retaliate. In fact, under the tree that day, David determined that he would trust God in the midst of opposition and respond honorably despite unjust circumstances.

Unexpected Attacks

Warriors are often blindsided—not by the enemy, but by soldiers in their ranks that claim to fight for the same cause. This is indescribable to me, and reprehensible. However, many times the hostility that rises from soldiers flying the same colors is more intense and aggressive than the stated enemy.

Naivety says that persecution should come from the outside, not from within. Enemies, not brothers, should insult and attack. Community should offer protection, not strife.

But, reality offers an uncomfortable truth.

Many times, the people that should protect us harass instead. Those that should build, destroy. And relationships that should support, oppose. The question remains. Why? Why does opposition come from within?

Many theories have been posed. The reason varies from situation to situation and person to person; however, there are a few core dissipations that routinely contribute to these illogical and destructive outbursts.

Jealousy does strange things to people. Instead of seeing his throne as the benefactor of David's exploits, it was jealousy that convinced Saul the victories were stealing his own glory. His jealousy drove a wedge between the king and his most loyal subject.

Afraid that the loyalties of the kingdom were being shifted to David, Saul's *insecurity* revealed itself. Logic flew out the window and the spear sailed through the air. When he felt threatened in his position as king, Saul let fly.

The *selfishness* in Saul could not handle sharing affections with David. When two of his children showed commitment to his one-time companion, a rivalry was birthed. As Jonathan (Saul's son) embraced David as brother, and Mical (his daughter) loved David as her husband, Saul's indignity grew.

Although many other things could have contributed to Saul's change in demeanor, I believe the strongest contributor was Saul's realization that the *Lord's allegiance* had changed. When Saul sensed the hand of God resting upon him in a way that sent enemies running and invited great blessing, he was content; he was more trusting, friendly, and at peace. However, as the Lord began to remove his favor from Saul and it tangibly rested upon David, Saul could not handle it. The sense of loss and alienation that was associated with the transition would have been paralyzing had it not been so infuriating.

Just as Saul may have been driven by jealousy, insecurity, selfishness, or awareness that God's favor had left him and was resting on another, so human nature drives others (even Christians) to do hurtful things and make wounding statements as they begin to lose control.

As a young warrior begins to experience God's favor, immature believers may lash out and attack him/her verbally. Occasionally, there are more extreme cases where division is so swift, opposition so defined, and the ambush so personal that the would-be warrior is left reeling as he tries to deal with his friend-turned foe.

You Have Been Served

Because I consider myself to be an easygoing guy who will bend over backwards to accommodate

and help anyone, I never pictured a time when someone would want to sue me.

"However, in my naivety, I did not understand that opposition is impossible to avoid."

Because I live a "turn the other cheek" lifestyle, and rarely demand to be right, innocently, I assumed that I could defuse every negative situation and turn potentially harmful circumstances into productive ones. However, in my naivety, I did not understand that opposition in impossible to avoid.

The saying goes, *"Keep your friends close... and your enemies closer."* I learned the hard way that sometimes your closest friends can turn into your impossible-to-ignore enemies. Those attacks can catch you off guard.

Out of a desire to help a friend, I offered him a job a couple of years ago. Sure, there were some self-ish motives involved in this hire (I felt that he could do a quality job and help our ministry in an area where we were understaffed), but one of the main reasons that I was inviting him to be a part of our team was to help him find a protected place to invest his gifts.

I had known Cameron for over three years. Although we lived in different states, we had built a relationship talking on the phone. I had also invited him to travel with me to some ministry events.

During that time, he seemed as if he was always searching for something to bring more meaning to his life. He had been called to ministry as a teenager, but after a couple of bad experiences in churches where he did not receive support, protection, or appreciation, he entered into the business world where he built a successful life.

However, that is not where his heart was. His dialogue was laced with longing. He wanted to be in vocational ministry. He wanted to directly affect lives through proclaiming Jesus to a generation.

Because our heart beat the same in that manner, as we began to look for another key team member to join our charge, I sat down and wrote a job description with his gifts, talents, and passions in mind. After a series of interviews and conversations, we offered him the job.

Early on in our occupational relationship, it was obvious that we were better friends than we were co-workers. We butted heads regularly over meaningful things as well as some not so important. The tension at the office was extreme, but we kept moving forward under the assumption that it would get easier as we adjusted to new dynamics.

However, things did not improve.

He told me multiple times in the first few months that he *"was miserable"* working for me. Dissatisfied with my leadership style, he lashed out, attacking my character. Once even referring to me as a *"jerk."* It did not take me long to figure out that I had hired him emotionally. Out of my desire to help him, I had missed red flags that the Lord had sent my way.

Trying to rectify the situation, we had a conversation, which led to him offering me a letter of resignation. Although he was angry with me, I felt that it was in the best interest of the ministry, our friendship, and his family, if he began to look for something that would satisfy him, in an environment where he respected the leader and believed in the mission. Desiring to bless him and his family, we offered him a severance package and prayed God would lead him into his perfect will. That is when it turned nasty.

After a series of letters and conversations trying to get more money, we were shocked to receive a letter from an attorney threatening a lawsuit. Confused, frustrated, and appalled, I did not know what to think.

"How can this guy that I have known for years, try to sue me? I tried to help this guy—to offer him someplace to join a team with a meaningful mission—how can he do this to me?"

For weeks, as we walked through this sticky situation, I sought answers that failed to come. Attacks were expected from the secular community, but not from within.

I would love to tell you that Cameron and I have made up and that a friendship on the rocks has been saved, but truthfully, I cannot say that. I continue to be befuddled by how something with such pure intentions turned so hideous, and I remain hopeful that one day Cameron and I will be able to have a cup off coffee together as we realize that we can accomplish more for our King if we lay aside our differences and work together. However, until that day comes (I pray that it will be soon), I have decided to learn what I can from the situation and grow stronger from it.

I am now wide-eyed and aware that division will come from every angle possible.

In order to slow the pace of the vision pursuer, the enemy will inspire even faithful friends as he works to drive a wedge, get attention off of the goal, and subvert God-given vision.

"I am now wide-eyed and aware that division will come from every angle possible."

As a warrior that dreams of winning battles for my King, I do my best to support those in the ranks, kindly and quickly dispel the aggressive actions of others, and fight only the enemy. As the spears fly through the air, I have to remind myself that God is the one that protects me. He has called me not to retaliate, but to forge ahead into the heart of the real battle.

Don't Lift a Finger

While hiding in the recesses of a cave hoping to go undiscovered, David and his faithful few were shocked when they heard rustling near the opening. After some investigation, it was reported that the spear-thrower had chosen their cave to *"relieve himself."*

Thinking he was alone, Saul disrobed and assumed the posture of a man...well...who needed relieving. Oh, the irony. Looking for a little privacy, the King had chosen a grotto...that was occupied by his archenemy.

David could have taken matters into his own hands and resolved his issue once and for all. He could have swiftly silenced his accuser. However, there was no blood on his blade as he crawled to the back of the cave...only remnants of the royal robe.

Instead of killing his adversary...he (*brutally*) cut a corner off of the King's coat. Instantly his conscience was stricken. He felt as if he had dishonored the Lord by lifting his hand in this small way against the authority of the land.

As his companions questioned him and urged him to return again to the mouth of the cave and take the life of the one trying to steal his, he refused. *"The Lord forbid that I should do such a thing to my master, the Lord's anointed."*

David chose to testify of his submission to God not with words, but with action. His example of trusting God to protect his reputation as well as his very life is a witness to all who face unjust accusations, persecution, and trials.

Until Saul fell on his sword in battle years later and ended his own life, David remained the hunted, but he never turned into the aggressor. Although his example contradicts culture, it coincides with the Bible's teaching.

God is the one who will avenge. Even when opposition arises from unexpected sources, God does not need your help. He will protect you. Even if the accusations are completely false, do not strike a pose of defense. Someone may try to destroy you and all God is doing through you, but there is no need to fear. God is with you...he will guard you.

David knew that God provides an inpenetratable shield. He is the impossible-to-conquer strong tower. He is your counsel, witness, and defense. Even if storms brew and wars rage, with God on your side, nothing can harm you.

Question is...how will you Respond?

As an aggressive believer steps out with weapons of righteousness and vision in hand, those of the same sect but with less fire commonly discourage them. Ready to impact the culture and live by a higher standard, determined Christians set out to advance the King's purpose and fulfill his edicts, yet support comes slowly—sometimes never at all. In its place, criticism, accusation, and judgment.

If an overly-aggressive response is offered, poor character is exposed. If a war of the words begins, a chink in the armor is revealed. However, if the attack leads the would-be-warrior to run to Christ for protection, understanding, and peace, their foundation is strong, and they bring a smile to the Lord.

Remember in the Bible when God bragged about David saying that he was "*a man after his own heart*"? Could that statement have been derived from his response to the spear?

Could the strongest statement about David's character have been, not his faith as he faced Goliath, but his reaction to Saul's assault?

David had a strong conviction about protecting authority, trusting God with the outcome of many serious attacks, and only fighting battles that were inspired by God.

He showed us *The Warrior Way.* We would be wise to mimic his attitudes and duplicate his actions.

Chapter Thirteen

Opposition: Unexpected Attacks

Thought For The Day:

Attacks may come, but God is always with you.

Scripture Theme:

Psalm 55:12–14 "If an enemy were insulting me, I could endure it; If a foe were raising himself against me, I would hide from him. But it is you, a man like myself, my companion, my close friend, with whom I once enjoyed sweet fellowship as we walked with the throng at the house of God. "

Questions To Ponder:

Do the unexpected attacks render you helpless or do they teach you to stand firm in the face of opposition?

Do you advance on your own when you feel as though you have been wounded or do you wait like David did and choose to see God's will done?

Digging Deeper:

Saul turned on David in I Samuel 18 & 19.

CHAPTER 14

Worship: Undignified And Proud

My perception of a worshiper has changed dramatically over the years. Although my attitudes were subtle and hidden, I used to assume that people who were uninhibited in worship were not connected to reality.

I could not relate to the artsy musicians who filled my pictures, nor did I want to. Those with extravagant affection did not seem balanced. Floating from emotional to flaky, these perceived characters related to everything through feelings and used flowery language that seemed unrealistic.

However, after I spent time studying the life and worship habits of David, the shepherd-turned-warrior-turned king, he destroyed my preconceived notions and redefined the depiction of what a radical worshiper looks like.

A valiant warrior to the core, yet a visible worshiper, he penned these words, *"But I, by your great mercy, will come into your house; in reverence will I bow down toward your holy temple"* (Psalm 5:7). David did not run from bloody battles, yet he spoke romantically about and to his God. *"O God, you are my God, earnestly I seek you; my soul thirsts for you, my body longs for you, in a dry and weary land where there is no water"* (Psalm 63:1).

He was not intimidated by any enemy; yet he had great reverence for the Lord of Heaven, actually declaring, *"The fear of the Lord is pure, enduring forever"* (Psalm 19:9).

The same young man who confidently engaged Goliath knew that a relationship with God was an undeserved privilege. *"What is man that you are mindful of him, the son of man that you care for him?"* (Psalm 8:4).

Worship fueled David's efforts and shaped his attitudes. The revelation of the indescribable beauty, unlimited faithfulness, mighty power, and personal love of the Creator captivated and empowered him. *"For great is your love, higher than the heavens; your faithfulness reaches to the skies"* (Psalm 108:4).

I could go on for pages rehearsing David's worship, but one particular biblical example outlines David's obsession with God. If you visit II Samuel chapter 6, you can take a peak at perhaps the greatest worshiper/warrior the world has ever known.

Obsessed... Extravagant... Radical... Unashamed...Fanatical...Passionate. All of these words paint a descriptive picture of David's attitude toward worship and his style. But the word he used to describe himself was *"Undignified."*

While transporting the Ark of Lord's Presence to his hometown, David got lost in a worship encounter unlike any that I have ever experienced. So consumed with the thought of honoring God all along the way, the king required the parade to stop every six feet in order to sacrifice.

But his actions were not religious and rigid; they were free and celebratory. David danced the entire way. Violent movements intended to please the heavenly audience came as this warrior *"danced before the Lord with all his might"* (v. 14).

"With ALL his might!" Can you imagine what that must have looked like? A grown man, an accomplished warrior, and the reigning king exercising no restraint. He offered every bit of energy and passion that he had to rejoice in the goodness of God.

Although others surrounding the spectacle joined in with shouts and trumpet blasts, their expressions of worship helped them fit in; David's made him stand out. Knowing that true worship only takes place when you lay aside every bit of pretense and human accomplishment, David did not dance as the king. Replacing his kingly robes with a linen ephod (a priestly garment reserved for those who served before the Lord; typically, a close-fitting sleeveless pullover about hip length), he proclaimed to all who were watching that day his adoration for God and his dependence upon him.

Surprise filled the hearts of his nobles. Perhaps some were uncomfortable at his generous offerings of unashamed delight. But he did not stop. Even when his wife attempted to bring a rebuke declaring that his behavior was unbecoming for a king, he did not retreat. Instead, he threw out that word. *"I will become even more UNDIGNIFIED than this"* (v. 22).

In effect, he was saying, *"I'm just getting started. When I worship I will not be concerned with what someone else thinks about me. I will not be reserved. I will not consider my position or my post. No! When it comes time to glorify and honor the God of Heaven, I will focus solely on Him. Joyfully, I will give him all of my energy, intensity, and zeal."*

As you can see, worship was as much a part of David's life as war was. He discovered the courage to enter fields of battle through his times of focused worship.

And he worshiped because he learned on the field of battle that God is *bigger* than his enemies were *bad,* and *better* than they were *big.*

The worshiper and the warrior became inseparable. He was defined by both. He would not have been the successful soldier that he was, had he not also been the undignified worshiper. It was his lifestyle of and his commitment to worship that shaped him and molded him into the aggressive fighter for godly causes that we read about and admire. This same principle has proven itself in my life as well.

"The worshiper and the warrior became inseparable."

As a young youth minister, I did not handle adversity well. When a crisis arose or when something went against my plans, I would become sullen—angry, even. Although I thought I hid it well, when our bus broke down on the way to a youth convention, I realized that my students were whispering about how irritated I was and were going out of their way to avoid me. I did not lash out at anyone, but the expressions on my face revealed the anxiety in my heart. This grieved me.

The fear and concern I saw in their eyes haunted me—I realized it had been caused by my emotional immaturity (yes, I believe that most anger comes from emotional immaturity) and smoldering frustration. This was not acceptable. I resolved to pray.

Over the next couple of days, I snuck away from the chaos of activity that surrounded the event, and I began to ask God to take control of these areas of my life. *"God, I don't like the immature emotions that dominate my life, steal my peace, and scare my students. Please help me overcome them."*

Strange came the reply. He did not rebuke me or my attitudes. He did not rehearse my mistakes; instead, he spoke to me about worship. I walked away from those moments with God convinced that the Lord was asking me to build a habit of worship.

Not understanding why he ignored my issues with anger/frustration in order to evaluate my dedication to private worship, but wanting to be obedient, I resolved to invest some money on praise music and devote time to building a lifestyle of worship. From that moment on, I began to prioritize this practice.

Although I did not feel the transformation taking place, something indescribable but truly wonderful changed *inside* of me…and I recognized it several months later. I realized it in the midst of a crisis.

While embarking on a ministry tour with a band made up of four of my friends, we hit some bad weather in Nevada, and I rolled our Suburban.

As we had begun to climb into the mountains in the northern part of the state, I hit some black ice that sent my vehicle angling strangely toward a ditch. As the two right tires hit gravel, the top-heavy vehicle loaded down with musical equipment made three-and-a-half rotations before it came to a stop. (We know that it was three-and-a-half because Andy, the drummer, kept his eyes open and counted the revolutions. The police confirmed it later that day.)

My mind was slightly hazy when the vehicle finally came to a stop. I was not dizzy as much, as I was living between reality and that place where you feel as if you are in a dream. After a few minutes, I climbed out of the broken driver-side window into the cold air.

As I stood there with a light snow falling on my face, I did not freak out. Actually, the opposite was true. I calmly began to sing—and not an "*I just rolled my Suburban song*"—there are none. From somewhere spontaneous, I began to sing to the Lord.

With my eyes closed and my fists clenched, "*Let your mercies fall from heaven. Sweet mercies fall from heaven.*"

After three or four lines, I was interrupted by Dan. "*What are you doing? Do you understand that you almost killed us?*"

Something was different in me. Instead of looking at all of the equipment, thinking about the church

215

services we were going to miss or worrying about how we were going to get home, my first response in the midst of a major crises was to think about Christ and his goodness.

Shortly after that, I began to count heads. Nate was walking toward me with blood dripping down his arm (from where he had flown through his window), holding his side. Marvin also came holding his side, while Dan and Andy did not appear to be injured. Unknown to me, blood was dripping down my head from where the windshield and roof of the vehicle had made contact. Things did not look good on many levels, but no one in our group became discouraged (except Dan).

Because we were out in the middle of nowhere, we needed a place we could go and wait for the ambulance. After a couple of fruitless tries, we found a farmhouse willing to let us make the call and hang out.

We were told it would be two hours before the paramedics would arrive, so the family who invited us in made some soup and bread. After we ate I realized that the blood around my eyes was starting to dry, making it uncomfortable to blink, so I went into the restroom to clean it off. As I looked into the mirror I noticed a twig sticking out of my eyebrow. *"Cool, souvenir."* So I popped it out and took it home to my wife (she did not appreciate the gesture).

At that point, the story gets humorous. (As I relate it to you, you may think I am exaggerating, but I have confirmed the details with those who were with me; and they will gladly back everything I am about to tell you.)

After two hours the ambulance showed up. Because they had experienced a long day running from one accident to another, they came with weary expressions, short fuses, and bad bedside manners.

Their dispositions were discouraging, but their competence left something to be desired as well—they didn't even have enough gas in the ambulance to get us back to the hospital. They drove 10 miles out of the way to buy fuel. With us in the vehicle, they had to stop for gas...and I think the driver bought a Mars Bar.

When our heroes (can you sense the sarcasm?) arrived, they began to look us over and ask us questions. While feeling my back and neck, I was asked, *"Where were you sitting...what happened to you?"*

"I was in the driver's seat, and I feel fine except that my head got crushed a little."

"Oh, so it's your fault," was the reply.

"I guess so," I chuckled.

"Well, we want to strap you down and take you in so we can check out your neck and spine."

"Do you really have to strap me down?" I said. *"It has been two hours, and I feel fine."*

"Sir," she replied with no facial expression at all, *"with the mechanism of your injury, you could crash on us at any minute and we want to be prepared."*

"So even though I feel fine, I could die?"

"It has happened." She shrugged. *"Why don't you head on out to the ambulance, and we will strap you down out there."*

Forcefully voicing one of the few things I know about medical procedures, I spouted, *"Maam, don't I get a ride on a gurney? I thought if I had a possible neck or spine injury, I wasn't supposed to walk anywhere."*

I couldn't believe her reply. *"Sir, it's been two hours."*

In slight rebellion, I picked up a suitcase and a guitar and walked out to the vehicle, laughing under my breath.

They loaded all of us into the ambulance. Five of us, three paramedics, luggage, guitars, amps... They strapped Nate to a board and put him on the left side, strapped me down in the middle. They put oxygen tubes in our noses and never turned them on—Nate said he did not feel any flow. They related it to an airplane where air was flowing, but it was not noticeable; however, when they got us to the hospital and plugged the oxygen into the wall, Nate noticed a difference and said, *"That was never on."*

They put an IV in Nate. Then because they had run out of normal-sized needles, they used one three times as big for my arm. I did not feel it, but I saw it. A rainbow of my own blood shot across my body.

Everything they did was comical.

As the angry paramedic began to clean blood out of my hair, I could feel her rubbing the glass into my scalp. It was cutting into my head and cutting off my hair. With locks of my hair falling down my face, I asked, *"Did I make you mad?"*

"No, why?" she asked.

"Because you are hurting me."

For over an hour we were in the ambulance, but never once did hopelessness or discouragement enter into my mind. Anger did not visit—instead, I reverted back to worship.

For absolutely no logical reason, I drifted off to the place that I had discovered a few years back—that place where I stand in awe of God and all that he is. With my eyes closed and my fists clenched (I cannot explain why I gravitate toward this posture; it just comes naturally), I began to sing a song. I thought it was under my breath, but when I opened my eyes, I realized it had been audible.

"I can't get enough of you...for I am in love with you."

The look on the disgruntled paramedic indicated she thought I was singing to her. I stopped singing in time to hear her turn to Marvin and ask wryly, *"Is he always like this?...because with head injuries we sometimes look for changes in behavior."*

With amusement in his voice, he responded, *"Nope, he is always like that."*

Minutes later we arrived at the hospital. They wheeled me into the emergency room, put me in the back, and forgot about me for 45 minutes. During that time I became grateful. Not that I was alive (I did not realize that I should have died in that accident until we later visited the wreckage), but that my first response was to worship God.

Comparing my reaction with the one I would have had years back, I was pleased with the changes that had taken place in my life. Instead of seeing the circumstances, I looked for Christ—and I found him. He was waiting to offer me peace, hope, and assurance.

"Instead of seeing the circumstances, I looked for Christ—and I found him."

The habit of worship has strangely affected my life in visible ways. From that crisis in Nevada to other moments of stress, the times I have spent leaning on God and learning from him have offered me a grounding in God's goodness that has outweighed and overcome the circumstantial issues I have faced.

Perhaps more than anything else in my life, the worship I have willingly invested (sometimes it has been sacrificial praise expressed because I knew it was the right thing to do; other times, it has been free-flowing amazement expressed in moments of God-awe) into my life has developed in me faith and courage. Reverent offerings of thanks have reminded me that God is my deliverer and I am his child.

Bold declarations of his goodness have influenced my attitudes and behaviors chasing off doubt and unbelief. Meditations of God's faithfulness have convinced me that I will never be alone, nor will I ever be forgotten.

Moments spent in adoration (loving him for who he is) and admiration (acknowledging what he has done) have become a wonderful part of my daily life. They have stoked the fires of faith. They have imparted wisdom and perspective. And they have shaped my reactions and perceptions.

I know that the successes of my past have come, in large part, because I have made worship a priority. In the same way, I know that I will see more victories in the future because I will continue to contemplate his character, remember his faithfulness toward me, and linger with the God who is above all gods. I will continue to devote my life to worship.

I want to become more Obsessed, Extravagant, Radical, Unashamed, Fanatical, and Passionate. And in following the example of a great warrior, I am willing to become even more UNDIGNIFIED as I learn to worship my King.

Chapter Fourteen

Worship: Undignified and Proud

Thought For The Day:

> Worship when you don't feel like
> it and eventually you will.

Scripture Theme:

> I Peter 2:9 "But you are a chosen people, a holy nation, a
> people belonging to God, that you may declare praises of him
> who called you out of darkness into his wonderful light."

Questions To Ponder:

> Do you have an attitude of wor-
> ship when others are watching?
>
> Do you have an attitude of worship when the
> sky is falling and everything seems hopeless?
>
> How can you worship God with ALL that is within you?

Digging Deeper:

> II Samuel Chapter 6 records undignified worship.

CHAPTER 15

Temptation: Warriors Beware

Okay, let's talk about an issue that you must deal with if you are going to stand for truth and fight battles for the King—let's talk about temptation. More specifically, sexual temptation.

Whether you want to admit it or not, temptation is lurking in the shadows and it has its sights set on you. Temptation is a relentless, angry, and aggressive foe. Its goal is spiritual sabotage: it wants to knock you down and take you out.

It continually tries to set its fangs in the flesh of your faith in order to dominate and devastate God's work in you as well as the victories that he wants to win through you. If you allow its jaws to clench, the venom will release, beginning the process of belief deterioration and destiny destruction. And no, I'm not over-dramatizing this particular sin because your pastor, parents, or girlfriend wrote me a letter.

If you underestimate the power of temptation you are playing with fire. If you underestimate the power of *this* temptation, you are playing with nuclear weapons. You must be aware of its destruction in both your private and public life. For if you allow yourself to become convinced that sin can be controlled and covered up, it is just a matter of time until you realize that what is done in secrecy will be shouted from the rooftops, bringing embarrassment and humiliation.

You cannot go toe to toe with temptation—you must refuse to play his game. Temptation works in strategic steps aimed at softening your convictions and getting past the barriers that you have established. It can subtlety go unnoticed for a season, but eventually it rises up, revealing the authority that it has silently usurped.

Sin is not a one-step process. Every temptation is not distinctive and exclusive. Each one seeks to build on its predecessor's foundation, slowly adding more weight on the belt that will drag you down to the bottom of the sea. In order to keep your head above the water and continue to breathe, you must fight sin where it is conceived. To explain, let me tell you how temptation has visited me.

I was not born with sexual thoughts running through my mind. When I gulped my first breath and released my first scream, my body was covered with strange fluids, but my mind was pure. I did not recognize temptation at that young age: there was no attraction, appeal, or lust. However, as I began to age, images began to bombard my brain. The pictures on the billboards, sexual storylines in commercials and movies, and innuendo that surrounded me in my formative years all began to draw my attention to sexual things. Society worked hard to imbed those images deep inside of me. (Whose plan do you think that was?) However, I could have still maintained my innocence—IF I had protected myself as much as possible. That is where I went wrong.

At a time when my faith was comfortable and no spiritual attacks were evident, I let my guard down. I let my habit of daily getting close to Christ, reading His book, and fighting against the spiritual immaturities in my life disappear. In their place, I adopted an unspoken apathy.

Along with a complacent attitude towards spiritual investment, I adopted a casual outlook on sin. Instead of doing all that I could to avoid those images that steal innocence I invested them into my heart. Conscience (or is that the Spirit of God?) reminded me that I should avert my eyes, change the channel, and shut out the sexual conversations, but I allowed those things entrance into my heart and mind.

When I ignored the voice telling me to protect myself, temptation strengthened its hold. Convinced that my morals would win out and that I would never make shocking mistakes, I lived a double life. Surrendering to their evil desires, but keeping them hidden and tightly covered up, I thought that I was cleverly winning the game.

However, after time, the urges became stronger and my will weaker. The temptations that I used to be able to hide and visit only in moderation were taking up more of my time. And the games that I had to play to keep them hidden became more intense.

Slowly it happened. Sin was taking over, and my life was tragically affected. Although I had promised myself that I would not become like everyone else who was giving in to sin and drifting further from God, I was trapped in immorality. I was addicted to sin.

"However, after time, the urges became stronger and my will weaker."

At that point, I could no longer hide it. My addictions began to seep out in conversations and expose themselves in little ways. It was becoming more and more obvious that I was losing the battle with sexual thoughts, images, and actions. I even lost the ability to fight. I felt trapped. My safe and hidden sin was staring back at me every time that I looked into the mirror. Temptation was winning.

"The things that you set your affections on when you are alone will one day dominate your life when you are in public."

One day, while I was praying and pondering my life and the internal battles that I was facing with temptation and sin, I pulled out a post-it note and wrote down this profound statement. *"The things that you set your affections on when you are alone will one day dominate your life when you are in public."*

That statement has proven itself in my life. It is confirmed in the life of David as well. Although he beat Goliath and brutalized his enemies routinely, he lost an epic battle to temptation.

Check it out...

Many years had passed since David had fought and defeated Goliath. Saul was long gone, as were the spears that he had used to launch at David as the object of his jealousy and scorn. The early trials that kept David in hiding had run their course. Life had fallen into a relatively manageable pace for this shepherd turned king.

Jesse's son had fallen into a comfortable stretch of life where he thought he was safe.

Everything in David's life was shockingly great. That is when—and that is *WHY*—he made one of the most notable blunders of his life.

Although most kings will forever be remembered for their successes and failures in political realms, David's mistakes ensured that a significant part of his legacy would come from character weaknesses and poor choices in his personal life.

It was springtime in Jerusalem, a time when kings should go off to war. Either to fortify their empire or to take new territory, monarchs with kingdom responsibilities did not stay home. With aggressive postures kings went to battle.

But David did not. He remained near the comforts and conveniences of his palace.

Joab, the leader of the Israel's army went on a campaign, but not David. Why should he? There was no urgency. There was no threat. He was content. Satisfied. He was complacent. That is when the sniper of temptation and a poor decision found David vulnerable and pulled the trigger, bringing escalating, catastrophic, and embarrassing consequences on the king and his family.

Late one night, David lay in his royal chamber unable to sleep. We do not know why he struggled to drift off that night, but we do know that because he could not, he moved from his bed to the roof of his palace.

Walking in the moonlight, David found the edge of the roof wall and leaned against it. Looking with imaginative eyes past the flickering fire lights of the city, he pictured the camp in which his troops gathered. He considered his mighty men who he had fought beside many times, the men who made war out of loyalty to Israel, David, and the God that he served. He wondered what they were doing in that moment. Perhaps he imagined himself in the tent lending his expertise as the officers strategized about the next day's military activities.

Soon his mind began to wander and he left the tents of his soldiers and began to meander through time—to moments when fighting was imperative and war was inevitable. He remembered the adrenaline that accompanied his first battle. With pride, he recalled the shouts of adoration that attended the victory over Goliath. Many other campaigns followed.

The roof that night became a safe place to remember victories of the past and tributes that had been offered. It was a place where accolades were recalled and adoration was embraced fondly. As

David stood on the roof with his eyes scanning the horizon, the focus of his mind was not on the sand, stone, and mortar that were his present surroundings. Rather, his thoughts rehearsed the victories, accomplishments, and successes of his past.

"Temptation was bathing in the streets below."

That is when his eyes fell on…HER. Temptation was bathing in the streets below.

Shocked into the present by this vision, he quickly averted his eyes and wandered toward the other side of the roof. Because he knew he should not be consumed with the images of this naked beauty, he tried to block the pictures that had been seared into his conscience. He tried to find something else to focus on; however, he was losing the battle.

The image of this bathing splendor had followed him to the opposite side of the roof and was silently calling for him to come and take another gander. He had not come up to the roof looking for trouble, but trouble had come looking for him. And it found him.

It found him weak-willed, morally frail, and defenseless.

The accidental glimpse of Bathsheba in her tub was not a sin—a temptation perhaps, but not a sin. Sin did not enter the scene until David looked again and refused to look away.

After minutes of putting up a good fight, he finally caved. He slyly drifted back to the dangerous side of the roof. At the second glance he was trapped.

Minutes of intruding on her bath led him to act. He sent for her and had sex with her even though her husband was fulfilling his military duties. Rather than take responsibility for his actions when circumstances dictated that his indiscretions would be exposed, David tried to manipulate the situation and divert the blame. When that didn't work, he arranged to have the unsuspecting husband and loyal-to-the-end soldier killed in the line of duty.

After allowing her a time of grieving, he married Bathsheba, brought her into his house and tried to move forward as if nothing abnormal or immoral had taken place. *"But the thing David had done had displeased the Lord."*

His actions were uncharacteristic and unfit for any man of God. Especially one that had been promoted as a spiritual leader. However, the blemish on David's record did not begin on the roof. The attitude of complacency and contentment exposed him to temptation. Then the failure to look away led to drastic, life-changing, and legacy-impacting sin.

"The bigger the calling, the more aggressive the attack."

David's mistakes stand as a constant reminder that God's warriors are not immune from temptation. If anything, the ones that have great potential will experience the fury of sin's assault. The bigger the calling, the more aggressive the attack.

As willing warriors, we cannot allow temptation to win. We must fight against apathy, recognizing that our spiritual posture either protects us or leaves us vulnerable. We also must learn to protect our heart by posting a guard at the gateway (our eyes and ears).

Although in some games you can outshoot your opponent, a strong defense is your only hope against temptation. Let's take a look at the role that apathy plays in the battle against temptation.

In a previous book, *Bored with God,* I talked about how apathy affects lives and pulls them away from solid faith. My favorite quote from the book is, *"Spiritual apathy is the doorway through which sin enters and faith leaves."*

Someone once questioned me, saying, *"Isn't that too encompassing? You are blaming every negative in our spiritual lives on apathy."*

My response: *"I really believe that. Our spiritual posture—whether we pursue God or neglect Him—determines if we are strong or weak"*

Think about it. If the way that you approach God will either lead you toward Him or away from Him, what is your spiritual life going to look like in a few years? Will you be full of faith or full of fear? On-fire or lukewarm? Moral or immoral?

As a Christian, you have an exciting opportunity to pursue God. He will not hide from you. He is not the Wizard of Oz behind the curtain saying, *"Pay no attention to the man behind the curtain."* He wants to be found, but you have to move toward Him.

You can either devote yourself to spiritual disciplines and activities that have an eternal impact or you can waste your time living your life on things meaningless and trivial. If you go after God, you will not be disappointed. Your faith will be strong and your heart pure. However, if because of a calloused heart, a busy schedule, or a weary spirit you slow down, get knocked off your mark, and base your life around the whispered lies of invulnerability then you will grow weak, discouraged, and spiritually inactive.

Do you know what *"atrophy"* is or how it happens? Atrophy happens when something that was once strong becomes weak through inactivity. If you don't exercise your biceps, for example, then they will atrophy.

Protecting yourself from the atrophy caused by apathy is the first step; the second is guarding your heart. God encourages Christians to do just that, but what does that look like? In a society that is saturated with relentless images of lust, anger, immorality, and aggression, is it even possible to defend against the constant messages?

Although it is impossible to completely avoid all images and innuendos, you can maximize your protection by minimizing them. Simply put, you must adopt a strict stance about what you will allow into the gateways to your heart.

I got to a point where I knew that is what I had to do.

I know myself. In my life, one thing that I need to avoid is lustful images. I learned at an early age that one of the major ambushes that the enemy would use to sap my spiritual resolve and distract me was *"the female factor."* Because of that, I made a personal pledge to protect my eyes. I knew that by guarding my eyes I was guarding my heart.

Desiring to keep my mind and actions as pure as I can, I have avoided movies my friends didn't give a second thought about seeing. Although it hindered my social life, it enhanced my spiritual life. I also tried to be wise in the television shows I watched. And finally, I tried to be disciplined in the way I looked at girls.

Obviously, it wasn't always easy, but in order for me to be the man—the warrior—I wanted to be, it was necessary. Truthfully, I cannot say I won all of the battles. But because I realized that success in this matter was not optional—there was too much riding on it—even when I failed, I picked myself up off the mat, asked forgiveness, and renewed my heart for God, saying that I never wanted to lose sight of his will.

This brings me to an interesting point. Even if you destroy apathy in your life, and even if you protect your heart by learning to look away, you will still struggle. So, what will you do if (when) you stumble and fall? Will you use it as an excuse to go on a sin binge trying to find satisfaction in succumbing to temptation? Or, will you realize that you made a mistake, and ask God to forgive you and give you strength so you won't fall again?

Looking at David's life it is obvious that running to God, even after you have failed miserably, is the right thing to do. Although the blemish would remain, David's story did not end with hidden sin and a refusal to repent.

Sometime after his history had proven that this *"man after God's heart"* (God called him) could become a culprit of adultery and murder, God sent a messenger of truth to him. Using a cleverly crafted story to speak of the injustice that had been done and the king's power that had been immorally leveraged, the prophet Nathan revealed to the king that God was displeased with his actions.

Faced with an opportunity to feel sorrow and turn back to God or rebel, David declared, *"I have sinned against the Lord."*

True to his character, God's forgiveness flowed. Being the God of multiple chances who gives his people every opportunity to acknowledge their sin and return to their convictions, God pardoned David.

Consequences are often unavoidable. (Even when God offers forgiveness and it is accepted, sin often comes with natural penalties.) For David, family chaos ensued. But history still proved that God loved David and David loved God. Even after these horrific consequences.

His story teaches us to avoid apathy, guard the gateway to our heart, flee the evil desires of youth, and return quickly to the Lord when we stumble. None of us are immune to the lures of temptation. That is why it is imperative that we learn to fight it violently and respond correctly.

Only a portion of a warrior's legend will be told on the field of battle; a large slice will be revealed to be relived time and again as character and convictions are attacked by wily and seductive temptations. If self-control wins over weak will, and wisdom leads away from the ambushes, spiritual sabotage and destiny destruction can be averted.

If you want your story to be a testimony instead of a tragedy you must not wander around on the rooftop of lethargy. You must force yourself to look away as temptation on parade seeks to captivate your attention. And, you must quickly return to your convictions if you find yourself slipping.

As I said earlier, temptation has its sights set on you. Will the warrior in you only succumb to it in an occasional battle, or will you choose to let it win the war?

Chapter Fifteen

Temptation: Warriors Beware

Thought For The Day:

Sin leads to death....Holiness leads to life.

Scripture Theme:

I Corinthians 10:13 "No temptation has seized you except what is common to man. And God is faithful; he will not let you be tempted beyond what you can bear. But when you are tempted, he will provide a way out so that you can stand up under it."

Questions To Ponder:

In what part of your life do you notice apathy?

Do you run from temptation or do you dwell in its seduction?

Digging Deeper:

To read in more detail about this incredible story of David's mishaps and cover-ups followed by the confrontation you can read I Samuel 11 and Psalm 51.

CHAPTER 16

Pride: Poison Of The Soul

Pride and insecurity are polar opposites—yet they often express themselves in similar ways and many times coexist. Although the balance between the two is desired humility, rarely do I rest there. Irrationally, I tend to lean towards one of the excesses.

There are seasons in ministry where I question my calling and try to talk God out of his plan for my life. And, there are other times when I allow pride to sneak in and inflate my ego. When God grants me success, it can go to my head. When his favor opens great doors, I can feel (and act) as if I deserve them without any real sense of gratitude.

In the situations where I allow myself to become puffed up, take credit for the wonderful work of God's Spirit, or simply become proud of who I am in comparison with others less "*mature,*" I sense God's favor withdraw, his anointing subside, and the urgency of his correction increase.

When pride sneaks into my life, doors begin to close, blessings are less visible, and my labor intensifies. It is as if I am working twice as hard and experiencing a very small reward. Why is that? I believe it is because of one simple principle found throughout scripture that states: *"God opposes the proud but gives grace to the humble"* I Peter 5:5b.

When pride is allowed to exist in my life, I try to do "*business as usual,*" but find myself fighting against God himself. It is not that he does not love me when conceit is present. It is that he loves me too much to allow me to move through life with this subtle poison coursing through my veins.

From his cosmic perspective, he recognizes that arrogance becomes an opening in the armor of my character that can let in the most dangerous and destructive of weapons.

A Critical Spirit

When I began to receive attention because of the great things God was doing in my ministry, pride began to sneak in, but I did not recognize it.

Its silent but deadly seduction began as the youth ministry I was leading experienced explosive growth. Looking back, I now realize that God had me in the right place at the right time all he needed me to do was get out of the way so that he could be seen and draw young people to him. However, in the heat of the encounter, I became inflated.

Ironically, it was not that I was convincing myself of how great I was—others were doing it for me.

Students were attaching themselves to me, professing how I had saved their lives (with a false humility, I would utter some rehearsed mantra such as *"No, son, God saved your life"*). Parents were attributing improved grades, better home lives, and fewer disciplinary problems to my involvement with their teens. Even the principle of a school told me how he had noticed a difference in the overall atmosphere of the school since I had arrived, stating that Christians were having more of an influence.

However, the real kicker came as I began to receive phone calls from youth pastors all over the nation asking me how we were building our program so quickly.

As time progressed, my attitude began to shift. I began to believe "my press clippings." I started to take credit. Pride began to swell.

"I still looked the same, sounded the same, and acted the same, but inside, my ego was outgrowing my spiritual linchpins."

Because I always said the "humble" thing, I didn't even realize the poison was running its course. I still looked the same, sounded the same, and acted the same, but inside, my ego was outgrowing my spiritual linchpins.

Because pride is so subtle and it does not ambush you with visible weapons, before you realize it exists, it can be so rooted and entrenched in your attitudes, faith, and expressions you have a fight on your hands. That is what was happening to me.

The first year of ministry at this particular church, we saw hundreds of students come to Christ. High percentages of several local schools were attending our mid-week service. Everyone knew about our group, our passion for Christ, and our desire to live our authentic faith aggressively. However, somewhere along the way—the momentum left. The flood of new young people stopped coming.

We were no longer the "*bell of the ball*" or the "*talk of town.*" Whereas everyone had heard about what God was doing with our group before, the whispers had subsided. Our influence was dwindling and our impact was missing. About that time, I realized that many of my attitudes were angry and arrogant.

When talking with certain ministry friends I felt free to share my strong opinions about anyone or anything that did not measure up to my level of perceived effectiveness. I began to spew negative venom when discussing preachers, churches, and even young Christians that were struggling. A trend began to repeat itself in my life where I became less caring and loving and much more critical.

Because I had not surrendered to the *"dark side"* of cynicism and sarcasm, whenever the comments would leave my mouth, I would see them rise like a vapor of rancid bile; but I could not get them back. Although I was grieved at my lack of compassion and ever-increasing judgmental attitudes, I was entrenched in the murky stream of negativism.

As time progressed, my sarcasm became more cutting, opinions more jaded, and my attitudes increasingly haughty. I was trapped in a cycle of regret. Whenever I would offer one of my biting commentaries that grew out of my *"I could do it better than you"* worldview, I would immediately experience a pang of guilt. The remorse in itself thrust me back into the defensive comments intended to rationalize my original statements. My experience taught me that a critical spirit is one of the most common ways that pride expresses itself.

There I sat in a ministry that was visibly watching the favor of God begin to dwindle and all I could do was recognize other people's faults. The joy of my faith journey and the exhilaration of being used by God to speak into lives as I fulfilled my calling were beginning to disappear. The God-intoxicated adrenaline that used to exist as I would see students encounter Christ in a life-altering way had been replaced by a weary soul that was struggling for its survival.

"This poison had infected my spiritual bloodstream and it was slowly stealing life, zeal, and perspective."

Pride had crept in. This poison had infected my spiritual bloodstream and it was slowly stealing life, zeal, and perspective. Ministry was difficult, relationships were harder than normal, and my relationship with Christ was at a standstill. I did not recognize it at the time, but I was in trouble. I was at a crossroads. If I did not wake from my ignorant slumber and recognize that glory-stealing pride had attached itself to my heart, I would forever be affected.

Brought Low

Ripped away from the freestyle life of frivolous living and leisure, at 16 years of age, Uzziah was transformed from a student to a ruler. In fear and trepidation, he set about leading the people of Israel. Knowing that he had to draw on God as his source, his reign began with him passionately and routinely seeking the Lord. As he did what was right in God's eyes and allowed the One True King to lead him, he found success in all that he did.

Military campaigns against the Philistines were successful and the walled cities of Gath, Jebesh, and Ashdod were defeated. Uzziah proved that not only could he defeat his enemies, but he could also take care of his people. He was known as a ruler that improved the condition of communities by building towers, digging cisterns, and employing people. During his reign, wealth was accumulated, esteem was strong, and confidence was present across the kingdom. That is why his name became famous.

People began to take notice of the young king that was shown favor by God. That is when—and that is why—the ending to his story is much different than the beginning.

As people began to take notice of his success and the favor that he had been shown, pride began to creep into his heart. He began to take credit for all that had been accomplished in his reign. Even though God had helped him by defeating his enemies, prospering his people, and blessing all that he touched, his perspective became skewed. His ego became inflated—and consequently, his world began to crumble.

With his outlook clouded so that wisdom could not be seen, he took his eyes off of heaven. He rationalized disobedience (another evidence of pride).

Even though his sin was evident in what appeared to be a spiritual display of godly pursuit, he ignored God's commands about the temple. He did not submit to the spiritual authority (yet another evidence) that had been established by God, and the consequence was severe.

As he stood inside the temple preparing to burn incense to God, leprosy broke out on his forehead. As the skin ailment began to creep across his face, the priests ushered him out of the temple and into a place of spiritual loneliness, societal judgment, and royal banishment.

The day that pride took over his life, he traded his palace for a separate house, his health for a life of sickness, his defining relationship with God for one of struggle, and his godly legacy filled with success for one with life defining failure.

When he began to take credit, pride began to take root. As his fame spread, so did his ego. When he acted as if he were above God's rule and authority, something in Uzziah died. Favor was removed. Success halted. And the king began to suffer.

"When he began to take credit, pride began to take root."

The Glorified Life

The Bible makes it clear that *"Pride comes before a fall,"* but it also gives instructions about the posture that leads to blessing.

In I Peter 5:6, a promise is written that declares *"Humble yourself under God's mighty hand, that He may lift you up in due time."*

Although I had memorized this scripture as a young man (because I knew that humility was something that I longed to embrace), I lived it the only way I knew how, *"My way,"* which negated the purpose behind the promise.

Pride dominated my perceptions. Arrogance my thoughts. Because I knew better, I never voiced the *"I am better than you"* that I sensed in my heart, but my actions were driven by pride.

I was caught in between the reality that God wanted to bless me, use me, and promote me and the lie that my ideas were revolutionary, my gifts irreplaceable, my personality impressive, and my calling about me and me alone. The conceit ended up stealing time from my effectiveness.

For a short time, I was put on the shelf. Oh, God wanted to use me, but my attitude of arrogance forced him to let me sit and mellow for a time. Although I was doing the right things (reading God's Word, spending time in prayer, and sharing with others) I was struggling to connect with Christ.

When the internal irritation increased to the point where it became a constant companion illuminating unanswerable questions, I went into a time of focused and inquisitive prayer.

I began to call out to God. I had to discover the source of my disconnect.

Thankfully, God led me to a mirror and allowed me to see the pride that was wreaking havoc in my heart. My awe of God returned. The amazement that used to fill me was rekindled as I realized that he chose me to be his child—to be his ambassador even though I had nothing to offer.

My passion began to return—followed shortly by the personal presence of God in my life and his blessing in my activities. I would love to tell you that I won that battle and have never had to fight it again. But the truth is this is still one of the most consistent conversations that I have with God. I continue to battle my pride. I routinely fight off the critical spirit that tries to grip my heart.

Some days are better than others, but when I am reminded of the consequences and repercussions that I will experience if I let this poison win in my life, I cannot help but be diligent and militant.

Warriors will continue to fight against pride. They will let humility win in their lives. If they are to be all that God wants them to be, then they must overcome this silent, but infectious enemy.

The reality that warriors face is this: *with Christ, they can never be conquered.* But the key to walking in that type of authority, confidence, and certainty comes as they realize that *without him, they can do nothing.*

Chapter Sixteen

Pride: Poison Of The Soul

Thought for the Day:

> Humility is a quality that God honors
> and can promote.

Scripture Theme:

> I Peter 5:6 "Humble yourselves therefore, under God's
> mighty hand, that he may lift you up in due time."

Questions to Ponder:

> Do you have a critical spirit towards
> anyone or even towards yourself?
>
> In all of pride's forms, which one pres-
> ents itself to you the most?

Digging Deeper:

> II Chronicles 26 records Uzziah's prideful decline.

CHAPTER 17

Secrets: No Such Thing

The other night I had a disturbing dream. The most troubling part was not that I had traded my dedication to God and ministry for a life of crime; the worst part was that I was so bad at my newest pursuits (is that wrong for me to say?).

As I looked in on my life, I was a thief and a thug. One night when money was tight or boredom was intense, I went on a crime rampage with a couple of dark friends.

Being the intelligent and visionary criminals that we were, we did not rob banks, armored cars, or steal high profile jewelry. No…we held up pawn-shops—the mastermind equivalent of stealing from lemonade stands.

After three or four withdrawals, we ended up back at my home where we were greeted by a detective, quickly handcuffed, and led down to the station. Turns out that I was not a good thief—I left too many clues and got caught quickly. Things that were supposed to be shaded and concealed were left exposed.

As I woke from my sleep and rehearsed my dream, I could not help but laugh. I was amused that my mind had wandered to a place so foreign and that even in my fantasy, I was no good at keeping secrets. This is consistent with my history.

I got caught every time I tried to sneak into the house through the window as I tried to convince my parents I was in on time. Although I thought I could steal a cookie or snack without my mother's knowledge, the smudge of chocolate on my cheek or the evidence of the remaining wrapper would expose me time and again. Oh, I knew about the little ding on my parent's car, but I figured they would never see it. Again…I was wrong.

Exaggerations and deletions that were strategically intended to hide weakness, poor choices, or inconsistencies in my stories were always discovered. Eventually, the truth always came to the light.

"Skeletons hidden in closets will be aired for the world to see."

Although I tried to master the art, I was not good at deception. Want to know why? It is because there is a spiritual law declaring, *"There are no such things as secrets."* They don't exist. Skeletons hidden in closets will be aired for the world to see.

Oh…it is possible to hide certain things from certain people for a short period of time. But, eventually, all things will be exposed. What is done in secret (good, bad, or indifferent), will be known in public. And the secrets that are tucked away into the recesses of a person's life will end up defining him/her.

The Bible speaks clearly about this matter. *"There is nothing concealed that will not be disclosed, or hidden that will not be made known. What you have said in the dark will be heard in the daylight, and what you have whispered in the inner rooms will be proclaimed from the roofs"* Luke 12:2–3.

This is not just true when it comes to bad habits, immoral behavior, and hidden sins; it also pertains to godly pursuits, honorable behavior, positive investments, and wise choices made when one sneaks away from the activity of the world.

Jehu is a perfect example of this.

What Happened to you?

Jehu sat unsuspecting in league with his companions. Around the campfire sharing stories of battle, each of their hearts stirred with both dreams of power and questions of value. Each longed to lead armies, defend his country, and defeat its enemies. Yet, each was unsure of his destiny or his ability to leave an imprint on history.

For the most part, these dreams went unspoken, but when conversations turned to wars that needed to be waged and rivals that needed to be confronted, the gleam of vision was visible in their eyes. They longed to bring justice.

Their moments around the fire were always empowering. Collectively, the encouragement offered gave confidence and momentarily stripped doubt. However, when all was said and done, their vision of the future was trapped in their lack of activity.

But on this particular day, something changed. A message brought by an outsider changed the hierarchy in the group, inspired hope, and began a revolution.

They saw him coming from a distance. The thin frame of a man with his shirt tucked into his belt and carrying a large vial was running at a frantic pace toward the assembly. With curiosity peaked, Jehu and his company stood to greet the one approaching...the one recognized as a prophet-in-training.

"I have a message for you, Commander." (p. 204)

When he reached the group, he placed the flask he had been carrying on the ground, placed his hands on his knees, and spent a few moments capturing his breath. Then he spoke. *"I have a message for you, Commander."*

"Ok, let's hear it."

However, the prophet would not tell him. *"I have been instructed to get you away from your companions and take you into the inner chambers before I deliver this message."*

Although it seemed strange, and Jehu would have preferred to remain with his friends, he was interested enough in this promised message to draw into his tent.

Hoisting the flask off of the ground, the prophet followed him.

When both were inside the tent, the prophet popped the cork from the container and proceeded to pour the contents directly onto Jehu's head.

The thick oil ran down his hair onto his beard, saturating his clothes and dripping onto the ground. Jehu did not dare move, although the container filled with more than a gallon of oil took several seconds to empty.

Jehu recognized the significance of this demonstration. In stunned silence, he waited for the pronouncement.

"The Lord says that you are the new king of Israel. You have been prepared for this moment to step into this position and to lead this people. You must destroy the house of Ahab and bring justice to the evil queen Jezebel."

Then, before Jehu had an opportunity to respond, the prophet opened the door and ran, not stopping to explain what had just taken place to the commanders who waited outside.

With his hair and clothes still weighted down by the heavy load of oil that had been applied by the prophet, Jehu emerged from the inner chambers with a shocked look on his face.

As his friends turned to see him standing in the doorway, they smiled at the awkward sight.

Out of curiosity, one spoke. *"What happened in there?"*

Although there was no denying that something strange and dramatic had transpired, Jehu tried.

"Nothing, really. You know how crazy he is. He is always saying and doing strange things."

"That is a lie!" came the reply. *"You can't tell us that nothing happened. Look at you. You are drenched. He said something...He did something to you. You can't deny it. Tell us the truth."*

Looking into their eyes, he realized that he could not keep it a secret. What had taken place in the inner chambers was going to be made public; he broke down and gave them the news.

"The Lord said that I am to be the next king of Israel."

A spontaneous show of support followed. Jehu's companions all took off their coats and laid them on the steps. They blew trumpets and boldly declared, *"Jehu is King."*

What Happens in Vegas...

If you live in the United States, have a television, and don't click to a new channel the very second your favorite shows cut to a commercial, you can probably finish this statement. *"What happens in Vegas..."*

Although I do not want to comment on the message being promoted, I do want to share a biblical truth with you.

"What happens in the inner chambers DOES NOT stay in the inner chambers."

Here goes:

"What happens in the inner chambers DOES NOT stay in the inner chambers."

In our society, we would love to believe that it is possible to keep secrets...to live a double life...to hide certain things. Truthfully, however, you cannot. There are no secrets. What is done behind closed doors will be known to all. What is whispered when no one is around will be shouted from the rooftops. Veiled attitudes, hidden activities, and shadowy agendas will be exposed. When in college, I learned this the hard way.

I have never cheated on anyone that I have dated (in the worldly sense of the word); however, I did indulge in what I considered at the time to be harmless (as long as it was undiscovered) flirtations while in committed relationships. I would like to say that I was completely focused on the one whose picture was in my wallet, but truth be told, the attention and admiration of co-eds enticed me and led me to return playful banter.

Although I shrouded it with language that declared *"we are just friends,"* and knew that all the obvious playfulness must be veiled from those around, I would make excuses to be around a couple of these beauties and take pleasure in their interest.

Trina was one of those girls. She came to the college one semester after I did. And I noticed her right away (just because I was in a committed relationship with a girl in another state doesn't mean I can't enjoy the wonders of God's creation, right?).

When New Student Orientation began, young ladies from all over the West Coast were on campus; my single roommates told me to be on the lookout for the loves of their lives.

My perch behind the buffet at the college cafeteria allotted me the perfect opportunity to offer the services of my friends to give tours to the truly worthy recruits.

When Trina and Damaris (freshmen from Oregon) went through the line, we began a conversation. After they were finished eating, I made my way toward their table and offered to remove their trays. Obviously moved by the gesture of chivalry, when I returned and offered to show them around town with the help of Jonathan and Scott, they agreed.

That night six of us jumped into my car (making it very tight). Scott gravitated toward Trina, Jonathan toward Damaris, and I brought along Sherri (Jonathan's sister and a platonic friend) to hang out with to ensure even numbers.

Barely into the night, I began to notice Trina's gaze. When I glanced in the mirror, she was looking at me. Because she was beautiful, and because I loved attention, I was flattered.

When we stopped for dinner, she seemed to be flirting with me. Scott noticed it, too, so I tried to avoid responding in kind—but did not do a great job. When we were walking on the beach, Trina made sure she was near enough to hear my jokes—which evoked flirty laughter. That entire night I was ambushed by her charm—more truthfully, by the attention she gave me.

The next day the flirtation continued. For several days I tried to deny that I was intrigued by Trina's obvious interest, but the more she flirted, the less I resisted.

The following weekend, in the ultimate show of juvenile flirtation, I stole a stuffed bear out of her car's open window and proceeded to freeze it in a block of ice with only the head above the frosty surface. After a couple of ransom notes and a clever picture (she knew all along that I was the one who had her bear), I returned it to her.

Pretending to be mad, she made me vow to repay her for her emotional pain. We agreed that a car wash and dinner was adequate compensation (I was easy to manipulate).

In my ignorance, I thought my friends were also ignorant. I thought no one noticed the chemistry that was growing between the two of us. I held to my story that I was not attracted to Trina and that the time I was spending with her was time spent trying to applaud Scott's great qualities. However, I was living a lie. I was lying to myself and everyone else around me (nothing is sadder than to see someone who has been lying to others so long that he begins to believe the lies himself).

After dinner (we ate Chinese, by the way) we were sitting in her car talking, and I realized the trap that I had fallen into. I appreciated the attention that she had been showing me these past few days, but I had no intentions of stepping into a relationship with her. As I looked into her eyes, I could tell that she was buying the entire picture. She was envisioning our wedding day, our 2.3 children, our Beagle named "Brutus," the blue minivan parked in our two-car garage, and our white picket fence. She was falling, and it was my fault.

I started to freak out. Wanting to end the flirtation and get back to normalcy where I was concentrating on school and happily committed to my girlfriend, I tried to let her down easy. I started, "*You know, Trina, I think you are a wonderful and beautiful person, but I am already dating someone. If I weren't, you would definitely be someone that I would like to get to know better. But since I am attached, we need to be wise about how much time we spend together.*" After 20 minutes of additional conversation, we arrived back on campus with what I thought was an understanding.

The next day I realized that I was wrong. What she came away with from my *"letting you down easy"* speech was distorted. She heard me say that she was *"beautiful and wonderful"* and that although I was not available, I wanted to get to know her better.

She began to tell people on campus that we were beginning to date.

Everyone around me began to question my character. Sherri thought I was becoming a player (I wasn't; I was just plain stupid). Scott thought I was being an unfaithful friend. People I didn't even know began to question me aggressively and whisper as I would pass. Someone even called my long-distance love and told her that I was cheating on her (it could have been Trina).

What began as shadowy flirtation that I felt was innocent and invisible to others ended up defining me and causing me a great deal of difficulty. I was just having some fun basking in the admiration of a beautiful young lady; I never intended for it to go farther. However, the games, glances, and stolen moments needed lies to cover up (I first had to lie to myself and then those around me). Eventually, it all blew up in my face leaving me confused, frustrated, apologetic, and struggling to explain.

The secrets that I kept were not blatant; most of them were not verbal or self-recognized. But when the flashlight of truth and intention shined on them, I was left with a problem that took me weeks to dig out of and months to live down. What I rationalized, felt I could keep hidden, and sensed as harmless, proved to be dangerous and did not remain in the shadows.

Greasy or Oily?

If there are no such things as secrets, then we must be very careful with all of our activities—even when we think we are enjoying a private moment or indulging in a hidden pleasure. Time alone will either ensure spiritual strength and build character; it will dilute focus and power; or it will sap convictions, resolve, and eat away at integrity.

You can come out of solitude with the anointing of God, the glow of his presence, and the power of his Spirit on you; you can leave having neither invested into your faith nor affected it adversely; or, you can open closed doors and be dripping with the grease of sin, immorality, and poor choices.

See, the most important time in your day as it affects your faith and your destiny is not the time spent in church, with friends, or pursuing your education. The most important time is when you are alone. You will either invest your time on things that bring you closer to God, make you more like Christ, and prepare you for effective service; you will waste it, being consumed with meaningless entertainment and social activity; or, you will spend it dangerously on destructive pursuits.

The activities of the secret place will not remain hidden. The things done in solitude—the behaviors allowed—the habits formed—the affections indulged, will be known to all. There are no secrets.

What Jehu experienced in the inner chambers defined his life from there on out. What you do when you are alone will have the same effect. Because of that, doesn't it make sense to walk in truth, to live in the light, and to be wise when we are alone?

Warriors understand that nothing will remain in the shadows forever.

Chapter Seventeen

Secrets: No Such Thing

Thought For The Day:

The things that you set your affections on when you are alone will one day define your life in public.

Scripture Theme:

Luke 12:2-3 "There is nothing concealed that will not be disclosed, or hidden that will not be made known. What you have said in the dark will be heard in the daylight, and what you have whispered in the ear in the inner rooms will be proclaimed from the roofs."

Questions To Ponder:

Do you live one truthful life or are you divided by a secret life?

Would you be excited if all your secrets were aired for all to see?

Digging Deeper:

Read II Kings 9:1-13 to get a glimpse of Jehu's appointment.

CHAPTER 18

Compromise: Don't Make Peace

The world entices with seductive whispers that say, "*Live for yourself...get all you can...be the man,*" but God's voice counters those thoughts, "*Live for others...be vulnerable...show them MY love instead of YOUR might.*" We either live contradictory to man's systems and philosophies or we adopt them. Either we live by God's convictions that he has placed inside of us, or ignore them.

When faced with opportunities to compromise we either make war...or we make peace.

This morning I had the opportunity to make peace—ironically by throwing a punch.

While playing basketball at the local Rec center, the action became intense when I fouled a guy relatively hard. Although I did not intend to harm him, he misunderstood the aggressive nature of my actions. He turned around, lathered me with verbal jabs, placed his hand in my face, and shoved me toward the wall.

In the midst of the commotion, I wanted to retaliate. I wanted to push back...say something aggressive...or even throw a punch. However, I caught myself before I did anything stupid. I walked away and let him cool down.

As we left the floor a few minutes later, I began to think about my desire to retaliate...to lay him out...to hurt him in some way...to stand over him and gloat, highlighting his lack of size and skill in comparison to mine...but in the end, I was pleased that I had not responded more aggressively.

That moment was not about two basketball players...it was about two philosophies of life—two standards. That moment was about God's way (turn the other cheek and show kindness—even to those who don't deserve it) winning out over the world's way (swing first, ask questions later, and make sure no one pushes you around).

Obviously, there was a battle going on, but it was not between a writer and a mortgage consultant. No, the war was being fought between self-protection and self-denial for the sake of Christ.

See, the fact that I have surrendered to Jesus means that I have died to my selfish desires. Whenever that happens I live against the culture and make war on its system. If I had thrown a punch, I would have been compromising my convictions and my desire to be a testimony of God's goodness, grace, forgiveness, and mercy. I would have been making peace.

Godly warriors are not willing to make peace… just ask Jehu.

Compromise vs. Conviction

Shortly after Jehu received the news that he was king, he set out on a mission. He was going to destroy Ahab's family.

Not knowing how to interpret the news that a hoard of horsemen was converging on their community, the king (Ahab's son) sent a soldier to greet the company and discover their intentions. However, he never returned.

As the scout reached Jehu, he asked, *"Do you come in peace?"*

"What do you have to do with peace?" Jehu replied. *"Fall in behind me."*

Without hesitation, the soldier joined the charging army, changing allegiance from the king of compromise to the newly anointed king of conviction.

When he did not return, another was sent. Same question, same response.

"Do you come in peace?"

"What do you have to do with peace? Join me."

Another warrior left compromise and joined conviction.

Before long, two kings who had perpetuated practices that kept Israel from serving the Lord God were dead, and Jehu was out to finish what he started...he was out to confront Jezebel.

Upon hearing that Joram and Ahaziah were dead, Jezebel began to prepare to face Jehu. Although she sensed that death was her destiny, she *"painted her eyes"* and *"arranged her hair."* (Sometimes women defy definition.)

When Jehu entered the gate, she stood in the window and asked, *"Have you come in peace?"*

Not bothering to answer the queen of idolatry who had murdered prophets, Jehu asked, *"Who is on my side?"* Essentially, he was asking, *"Who is willing to make war on the loose morals, the blasphemous ideologies, and the ungodliness that has been dominating the landscape. Who is tired of making peace with compromise? Who is willing to embrace convictions and throw compromise out the window?"*

He found two such people. Tired of making peace, two eunuchs violently took action on their leader. They thrust Jezebel out the window. As Jezebel hit the ground, her blood splattered on the wall, and horses began to trample her under foot.

Although she was quite dead, God wasn't done with her. Turns out that he hates passivity so much that he was not willing to let the poster girl for compromised spirituality save face (you'll get the pun in just a minute). While Jehu and his companions were eating and drinking, dogs came and ate her flesh, licking her bones clean. Much of her body was actually carried off by the dogs. When the soldiers returned to bury this former princess, they found nothing except her skull, her hands, and her feet.

What an amazing (and somewhat gruesome) story highlighting the beginnings of a revolution. But there is more here than meets the eye.

Just as in my experience on the basketball court, this battle was not about two people, two rulers, or two monarchies—but two philosophies. Compromise had ruled the land for many years, but conviction had been building. Although the royals were worshipping idols, embracing immorality, ignoring

God, and rejecting truth, there were people who were ready for a change. The soldiers were ready to walk away from compromise and join the army of conviction. The eunuchs were tired of serving compromise; they were ready to put it to death.

When the missing piece came into view (an anointed warrior who had made a firm determination to stand for justice and truth), others joined the army. Conviction grew in strength, numbers, and passion; compromise went into hiding.

Don't Make Peace

If I want to be honest, I would have to say that before I was married I made peace with a couple of things that I should have fought hard against.

The Bible teaches that we are to *"flee the evil desires of youth,"* however, rather than run from those things, I tried to discover how I could experiment with certain sins while keeping my spiritual mask polished and my persona in place. I grew up with a strong conviction in my heart that I would protect my purity and hold fast to godliness. However, I failed to protect my heart early on from images and conversations that planted a dangerous seed in my soul.

"The seed was 'curiosity,' and over time, the seed became a vine that was strangling my faith and consuming my thoughts."

The seed was *"curiosity,"* and over time, the seed became a vine that was strangling my faith and consuming my thoughts. Although I tried to deny that sexual interest was growing (not an acceptable admission for a young Christian man), I could not escape the overwhelming questions that were always with me. Because sexuality was on display everywhere I looked and because conversations implied sex was the ultimate goal of life, these feelings that were tucked down into the shadowy recesses of my soul were growing. I was making peace with the culture's sexual agenda.

I created and began to execute a stealth plan that would allow me to experience the joys of sexual experimentation while continuing to protect my accepted and expected spiritual image. After coming up with a list of girls who met some pretty ungodly criteria (they could not be in my typical circle of friends, they had to be loose, and they had to like me), I began to contact them telling them I was looking for some experience without strings. Although I hate to reveal the depravity of my character, I am grateful to say that I could not go through with it.

It is not that I could not find anyone willing (the devil will always ensure that there is someone willing to lead you past temptation's threshold); something rose up in me.

The convictions about my purity returned… and shouted, *"I do not want to make peace!"* My faith returned reminding me that certain pleasures are temporary, but their consequences last longer. Confidence in God's laws resurfaced reestablishing my commitment to innocence.

"My faith returned reminding me that certain pleasures are temporary, but their consequences last longer."

That experience taught me that the seductive pull of temptation is unpredictable. At times, it is a frontal attack where the ambush is intense. Other times, your own thoughts work against you. Subtleties and rationales slowly break through your defenses and set you up for a fall. However, no matter the form that it takes, sin is still sin and compromise is still compromise. Whenever it whispers, you must not entertain it. Whenever it charges, you must stand. If it breaks through the defenses and wins a battle, you cannot roll over and let it win the war.

It is OK to Fight

"Turn the other cheek…"

"The meek shall inherit the earth…"

"Blessed are the peacemakers…"

The Bible regularly teaches that aggressive behavior toward another person is typically not the righteous course of action. However, there is one circumstance where God is not only pleased with hostility, he encourages it: God supports violence when it is aimed at compromise.

He does not want his people making peace with things that destroy their destiny and sap spiritual strength…he wants them to make war. Many would-be warriors never bask in the thrilling sense of victory…not because they don't have the tools to succeed, the skill to win the battles, or the knowledge necessary to make it to the winner's circle. Many lose the fight when they make peace with the subtle and seductive things that poison faith and render soldiers weak.

Some make peace with pornography, and the shame holds them hostage. Some make peace with immorality, and it steals their resolve. Others befriend bitterness and never notice their vitality leave and their frustration grow.

Still others slowly slip into a relationship with substances that are addictive, dangerous, and difficult to break ties with.

The opportunity will arise for every godly knight to make peace with something that can steal his power, dignity, confidence, or testimony. However, wise warriors who have enlisted for a lifetime of service and effectiveness will refuse to live in harmony with those things.

Radical Kingdom soldiers realize that they must make war on compromise in order to make peace with their destiny.

Chapter Eighteen

Compromise: Don't Make Peace

Thought For The Day:

> Live openly for Christ. Don't make
> peace with compromise.

Scripture Theme:

> II Timothy 2:22 "Flee the evil desires of youth, and
> pursue righteousness, faith, love and peace, along with
> those who call on the Lord out of a pure heart."

Questions To Ponder:

> In what area of your life are you
> making peace with compromise?
>
> Are you willing to fight for your convic-
> tions, for your future, for your character?

Digging Deeper:

> II Kings 9:14-37 records Jehu's
> attacks on Ahab's family.

CHAPTER 19

Passion: "I Will Not Be silent"

With confidence and conviction the words rose in the auditorium.

"I will not be silent,

I will not be quiet anymore."

As I looked into the eyes of the college students in the room that night, I recognized the anthem they were singing was more than a song. It was a declaration. Seven hundred strong were agreeing with the songwriter as they asserted their desire to live boldly, proclaim unashamedly, and live a life surrendered and useful to their commander.

The scene has embedded itself in my mind not because I simply like the song (although I really do); that picture is forever with me because I caught a glimpse of the passion that the emerging generation has to be used by God. The desire of those students was visible. They want to be mountain-movers, truth-proclaimers, narrow-path walkers, and sin-overcomers. They want to live for kingdom purposes and make eternal impact.

Young adults that understand the invitation Christ has offered them are not normal. They will not settle for a lukewarm faith and an apathetic approach to things spiritual. No, they are moving beyond casual Christianity as they embrace the lifestyle of the warrior. They are not satisfied to crack a Bible simply to fulfill a daily duty; they read it to catch glimpses of God's heart and to see his character fashioned in them. They long to live out the Scriptures that promise victory.

At the heart of their desires is a passion for God that drives them to live on purpose. They yearn to love what he loves. Hate what he hates. They want to align their lives with his plans (as opposed to have him bless theirs). This zeal that motivates them and will not allow them to slip into mediocrity also has another effect: It will not allow them to go quietly into the night.

People of passion cannot be silent. They refuse to ignore the subtle messages that destroy lives, and they do not have the ability to keep the life-altering love of God to themselves.

They are similar in design and expression to a New Testament revolutionary named Stephen.

"People of passion cannot be silent."

More Than a Waiter

By vocation, the first martyr of Christianity (after Jesus, of course) was a waiter. But the passion in his heart defined him as warrior.

Stephen had been picked by the apostles to help with the daily distribution of food. One of seven given the task so the leaders of the church could focus on the work of spreading the Good News and caring for spiritual needs, he had a servant's heart and a reputation as a faithful man.

The book of Acts records several accolades declaring that he was full of faith and the Holy Spirit, full of God's grace and power, and brimming with wisdom. As God worked through him, he did wonders and performed miraculous signs, and the opposition was unable to stand against his wisdom or the spirit by which he spoke. An impressive resume for a waiter and caretaker for widows, don't you think?

Whenever the Bible adamantly boasts about a person, I take notice. However, it is the brief glimpse we get into his fervent evangelistic efforts and his refusal to back down from opposition that catches my attention. Although antagonism had risen against Stephen because of the confidence he exhibited and the manifestations of heavenly might that followed him (his vocation did not define him; his position in Christ did), he did not let fear enter into his heart. Even though false accusations had been presented and punishment was being recommended, he would not defend himself. The persecution did not steal his focus. Instead of talk about himself or declare his innocence, he manipulated the conversation to talk about Christ.

Beginning with Abraham, Stephen walked through God's design for Israel and ended by rebuking those listening for putting to death prophets and the prophesied Messiah.

The mob grew furious.

This simple waiter refused to be quiet. When silence would have proven safer, the passion in his heart did not allow him to talk about things trivial or conform to what the throng wanted to hear. He professed what he knew to be true. Jesus was the one prophesied about long ago, and he had been unjustly crucified.

Gnashing their teeth, they charged. With their hands over their ears and yelling at the top of their lungs (this really happened), they attacked Stephen and dragged him out of town to stone him.

Even when the weapons of his own destruction were in hand, he spoke. Rather than live to speak another day, he released all that was in his heart. This waiter-turned warrior—this servant-turned-spokesman, experienced something amazing in return for his zeal.

As the stones began to beat against his body, he caught a glimpse of heaven. Jesus standing at the right hand of God was looking down on Stephen, approving of his unquenchable fire. The fervor that had infuriated the religious crowd had moved Jesus. He was standing and awaiting the arrival of the soldier of truth, proving that Jesus stands for anyone who takes a stand for him.

Before the stones had completed their task, Stephen fell to his knees and prayed that his murder would not be held against his assailants (talk about Christ-like). Then he *"fell asleep."*

Stephen could not be quiet. He refused to be silent. Even when circumstances dictated that he should decline comment, the urgency of the revelation in his heart would not allow him to do so.

"Indeed, I Cannot"

Jeremiah also had a passion that would not allow him to be silent. At one point, he penned these thoughts.

"His word is in my heart like a fire,

a fire shut up in my bones.

I am weary of holding it in.

Indeed, I cannot." (Jeremiah 20:9)

I have always wanted the intensity of the truth in my heart to make me uncomfortable and unwilling to ignore opportunities to herald it. One such situation surrounded me as I worked at a burger stand in my high school years.

The best burger place in Spokane is definitely Dick's Hamburgers. It is famous for its prices (it is unbelievably inexpensive) and its food. Although greasy, the burgers are exceptional. This was my first official job, and it proved to be one that tested my faith.

As I began working there, it was the first time in my life when I was forced to be around people that insisted on talking about sexual encounters and fantasies all of the time. Although I went to a public school, I could separate myself from a particular group or person if the conversation turned obscene. But when I was locked behind the counter for hours at a time and surrounded by this type of influence, I could not escape. I was captive to their stories.

The conversations occasionally turned spiritual as well; however, rarely in a healthy way. Knowing that I was a Christian, the jabs at my faith were routine. It was in this environment that I picked up the nickname, "Thumper," which had been shortened from "Bible-Thumper."

This atmosphere intimidated me on some levels. Some nights I found it difficult to hold onto joy in the midst of the minefield of immorality and the missiles of spiritual persecution. Knowing that I had an incredible opportunity to show the love of Christ in tangible ways, I worked hard to not be shocked when they talked of inappropriate things. I did not want them to feel judged (since that is what they expected from Christians), but I did not want to condone their ungodly activities either.

I was not against their sexual lifestyles, drug experimentation, and selfish living simply because it made me uncomfortable. I saw the effects on their lives. I watched as young girls were stripped of value and dignity as they got sucked into encounters with older guys out to conquer. I saw lives being destroyed by alcoholism. Although they thought their habits were harmless, I saw the destruction. I watched as some lost their jobs. Others destroyed marriages, and others hurt their future by ignoring their education.

As a Christian with an understanding that the rules God has established are not just whims but protective policies trying to ensure a fulfilling life, I wanted to speak up, but could not find the right way to do so. Every time I tried to initiate conversations about the satisfying life found in Christ, I would immediately get shot down. Sometimes the conversation would change; other times I was mocked.

The conflict in me grew. Knowing the freeing truth of God's love, acceptance, and personal plan, I grieved over their acceptance of lust-fulfilling behavior and reality-avoiding interests. Something inside of me wanted to speak, but I could not give voice to what was in my heart. That is, until Kelly started working there.

She joined the team at Dick's Hamburgers the summer before my junior year. Through a conversation in the break room, I discovered that she was a Christian. However, within the first month of her working there, she had adopted a new group of friends that included her in all of their dangerous activities.

"I saw another pure life being sucked into the vacuum of immorality and I was upset."

I watched as my new friend began to go out drinking three or four times a week. She started dating a guy who, by reputation, I knew would put undue sexual pressure on her. And I heard rumors that she had begun to experiment with marijuana. I saw another pure life being sucked into the vacuum of immorality and I was upset.

I was not angry with Kelly; I was furious that the lie of the worldly lifestyle was seducing its next victim. I knew that if I approached Kelly and tried to warn her about the guy she was dating and the partying lifestyle, she would consider me judgmental and prudish. So I did all that I knew to do. I prayed, asking God to protect Kelly and begging for wisdom to know how to help her.

Shortly after that, I had a plan. Without making a big fuss, I began to write Scripture verses on 3 by 5 cards and take them to work. Whenever there was a spare moment, I would pull one out, review it, and work on committing it to memory.

I had two purposes for doing this. First off, I believe that one of the best ways to ensure spiritual growth is to spend time focusing on God's Word. Second, I hoped that Kelly (and perhaps some other people) might want to memorize with me. I did not make a spectacle of my habit, but on the second day, Kelly saw me reviewing the cards in the break room and asked what I was doing.

When I shared that I was memorizing Scripture, she enthusiastically ripped the card out of my hand and declared that she was going to do the same.

For the next couple of weeks Kelly and I (and a couple of nominal believers along with one proclaimed atheist) memorized between three and five Scriptures every night that we worked. It was amazing. For me, it helped to connect with God's light in the darkest place that I had to frequent. And knowing that God's Word is powerful, I knew that something invisible was taking place in the lives of those who were participating.

This habit led to many incredible conversations at work about God's love, his mercy, forgiveness, his standards, and salvation. And, on a more personal level, Kelly's desire for Christ began to return. The prodigal took a good look in the mirror and realized how far she had fallen.

Sometimes Dick's Hamburgers was a place of trial and testing for me where I stuck out awkwardly. But as I found a way to give gentle (non-threatening) voice to my love for God, I discovered that there were other people searching who needed some encouragement.

"They fear silence that results in lives remaining in bondage and other lives being seduced into spiritual slavery."

Those twenty-somethings who declared their refusal to remain silent that night were giving voice to their strong desire to speak up—not because they have a selfish desire to be heard, but because they want God to be. They fear silence that results in lives remaining in bondage and other lives being seduced into spiritual slavery.

There are times when silence would be easier either because of the ridicule that they know will ensue or the frustration that will come as illuminated truth is ignored. However, the passion for God's principles and the dynamic power that backs his words do not allow people of passion to suppress what is in their heart.

Angry at the injustice, frustrated at the deceptions, with a heart for people, and a commitment to the message, warriors refuse to be silent.

Is it time you find your voice?

Chapter Nineteen

Passion: I Will Not Be Silent

Thought For The Day:

> May God never have to pry my mouth open
> to speak of his love and kindness.

Scripture Theme:

> Jeremiah 20:9 " But if I say, "I will not mention him or speak any
> more in his name," his word is in my heart like a fire, a fire shut
> up in my bones. I am weary of holding it in; indeed I cannot."

Questions To Ponder:

> Are you aggressively passionate for the
> Lord despite antagonists around you?
>
> Do you stand up for the cause like Stephen
> did, or do you shrink back in retreat letting
> the enemy gain territory that is not his?
>
> Will you be silent in lifestyle? Do others
> know that you are in Love with God?

Digging Deeper:

> Acts Chapter 7 is dedicated to Stephen's ministry,
> arrest, speech, death and vision of heaven.

CHAPTER 20

Purpose: Consuming Vision

Alone in the garden. Only yards away from eleven men that have walked with him through his ministry; he is awkwardly isolated. In the most intense moment of his 33 years, he is contemplating the shame and pain that await him.

The mob is on its way. The rugged cross has been prepared. The metal spikes that in a few hours would pierce his hands and feet had been chosen. Not only was physical abuse on the horizon, but abandonment unlike anything anyone had ever known.

The friends that he had rescued from aimless lives of mediocrity...the ones that he had loved and served were about to abandon him. One would violently deny that he even knew him.

However, the one thing that dominated his thoughts...that he could not escape from was the realization that his Father was going to turn away.

Up until that moment in time, he had always known the smile of the Father. He had sensed his light in the midst of darkness and his pleasure at all times. Stepping out of his glory in heaven was a lonely reality, but they still walked in perfect unity. The Son was with the Father. And, the Father was with the Son.

But, the agony that awaited Jesus would have to be experienced alone.

"But, the agony that awaited Jesus would have to be experienced alone."

Because God's holiness cannot bear sin, in one motion God would allow the sin of humanity (past, present, and future) to be placed upon the Son. As he did this, he would turn away.

Picturing the cold darkness that would sweep across the land and lay bare his soul, Jesus asked, "*Is there another way? If there is, don't do this."*

But, coming back to submission, he continued, *"Not my will but yours be done."*

In effect, he was declaring, *"The purpose that you have for my life is worth any amount of pain, discomfort, embarrassment, or agony that I will face. If my death helps you accomplish your goal, then I will willingly surrender."*

In that moment—when he surrendered his will, Jesus punctuated his life lived as a warrior.

High School Regrets

Have you ever known someone that was so strange that they stuck out like a sore thumb? The way they dressed? Their favorite topics of conversation? Their hobbies? Clayton was one of those guys

As one of my classmates in high school, he always drew attention, but it was never positive. Dubbed as one of the "*Ghost Busters*" (an assortment of the socially challenged, unathletic, and too-smart-for-their-own-good males who wandered around campus trying too hard to fit in and never succeeding), Clayton embraced his counter-cultural image. When everyone was spending big money and being defined by designer clothing, Clayton chose army fatigues and heavy-soled boots (before that look was vogue). Instead of speaking of common things, every conversation was laced with comments about fantasy games and militant activities.

Everything about Clayton was odd—so much so that he got picked on daily. His torture went from the mild mocking and giggling to the constant bumping and shoving that he endured as he would walk through the hall. Many times his books would get knocked to the ground. Other times some attention-seeking male would steal his backpack or glasses and run off with them forcing Clayton to charge after him down the hall.

For four years, I watched as Clayton struggled through the routine mistreatments. And, although he tried to pretend as if it was not affecting him adversely, occasionally, I got a glimpse into the wounded soul that he was lugging around day after day.

There were times that I felt sorry for him...even times when I prayed for him, but unfortunately I can not remember a time when I ever reached out to him and offered him my acceptance and Christ's love. Although I was readily aware of God's command to love the outcast (I could not read scriptures offering our commission without thinking of the "*Ghost Busters*"), I ignored it.

On many occasions, the conviction to reach out to him and others like him hit me hard, but I was not willing to surrender my will (and my reputation) in order to be God's hands and feet. I was not willing to endure the isolation from my typical crowd that would ensue.

"Looking back at my high school experience, I have come to regret the fact that I did nothing."

Looking back at my high school experience, I have come to regret the fact that I did nothing. I allowed Clayton and many others in my school to wander the halls questioning their value. Wondering if anyone cared. As I repaint the picture of those days and wish that I could go back in time and live it differently, I have come to realize just how egocentric I was. I longed to be perceived as smooth and together, but those people that I worked so religiously to impress are no longer a part of my life. The relationships that I embraced and protected at all costs remained shallow and meaningless, and disappeared at the first sign of tension or as soon as the diplomas were in hand, the tassels flipped, and the memories of graduation had faded. Yet, I chose them over God's will.

Unlike Jesus, I did not look at the wounded, the outcast, and the socially struggling and lay down my will to serve them. I chose self-protection and convenience while completely ignoring conviction's nudge. I was not willing to throw my lot in with them, but Jesus threw his in with me.

While we were still sinners with no redeeming qualities, Jesus gave up his will in order to fulfill that of the Father. For the sake of the broken, wounded, skeptical, disobedient, ignorant, and unworthy of humanity (which includes us all), he said, *"Not my will...but yours be done."* That declaration of surrender put into motion the literal sacrifice of his life.

He did not desire to suffer. There was no romance in the flogging that he received. No glory in the crown of thorns. No glamour as he hung on a cross, sustained in air by three spikes mounted as a hunting trophy for the world to see. His human will (like ours) was for self-protection. But God's will was that we would discover life through his death. Before his heart stopped beating and his body went limp, his will died—in the garden before the soldiers arrived.

If he crucified his will in order to win me, I am compelled to let mine die in order to advance his cause.

Chapter Twenty

Purpose: Consuming Vision

Thought For The Day:

There is no greater cost than that of Christ's.

Scripture Theme:

Luke 22:42 "Father, if you are willing, take this cup
from me; yet not my will, but yours be done."

Question To Ponder:

Do you live in surrender or do you
just visit once in a while?

Digging Deeper:

Jesus prayed in the garden and surrendered
his will in Luke 22:39-44.

CONCLUSION

Before the foundation of the earth, the plan was in place. In his infinite wisdom, God knew that the perfect relationship between man and his Creator would be interrupted by sin…he was prepared.

Before the first fish swam or the first dove fluttered, it had been determined that Jesus would lay down his divinity to fulfill God's ultimate purpose. He would be born of a virgin in a Bethlehem manger, be raised as the son of a carpenter, and grow in wisdom and stature. At the appropriate age (approximately 30 years), he would begin his public ministry. He would call twelve to his inner circle, perform wonderful miracles motivated by love, and teach with an impossible-to-ignore authority that would inspire thousands and infuriate the religious.

It was not just his life that was pre-ordained, but his death as well. God knew that his death would bring a revolution. The cross was the only way.

Pain must be endured.

Disgrace must be embraced.

Blood must be shed.

The goal was costly...always is.

Sacrifice was involved...always is.

But, the end result was worth all that was required.

Today...

Before the foundation of the earth, God knew you.

In his infinite wisdom God knew that the culture in which you would live was slipping towards spiritual apathy and moral depravity. He knew that the concept of absolute truth would be counterfeited and challenged, that his offer of limitless love for mankind would be scorned, that the slide towards corruption would gain momentum. Yet, he was not caught off guard.

Before the snake slithered in the garden or Noah hid from the initial drops of rain, it had been determined that you would live, that you would give your life for the cause of Christ, and that you lead a revolution. He knew where you would be born and to whom. He carefully sculpted your skill set, intentionally developed your personality, and creatively aligned your passions.

It was not just your existence that was pre-ordained, but your exploits as well. God knew that you have what it takes to live counter to the culture. To pray reforming prayers...to take transforming light into a shadowy culture...to lead an uprising. God called you to stand out by standing up...but it will not be easy.

Loneliness must be endured.
Excuses must be exterminated.
Insecurities must be overcome.
And, your will must be crucified.

The goal is lofty…it is time to bring Christ back into the culture. Sacrifice is involved…no worthy pursuit will allow you to remain comfortable. But the end result is worth all that is required.

"The goal is lofty…it is time to bring Christ back into the culture."

Christ will be lifted up.
People will know and respond to his love.
Society will be transformed.
Heaven will be populated, and the
gates of hell will be shaken.

With strong anticipation, the inhabitants of heaven have awaited your life. They cheer you on as a champion for your generation.

It is time to lead the charge.

It is time to make a difference.

It is time to pick up your sword, hit your knees, and engage the enemy.

It is time to embrace *The Warrior Way.*

Endorsements for *The Warrior Way*

"*The Warrior Way* is a very honest book. In an easy-to-read narrative style Sean Dunn interweaves his own life journey with stories of Biblical characters, drawing on his personal failures and victories to identify a broad range of issues facing any who want to be authentic followers of Jesus Christ. Dunn provides some poignant insights into the challenges and pitfalls that confront any Christian who wants to be an effective 'warrior' of Jesus and make a difference in this world. This book contains many treasures that will guide both the younger and older warrior through the snares and distractions than can so easily misdirect our path and take us on a journey to ineffectiveness, self-centeredness and mediocrity. *The Warrior Way* is a book that helps you understand your unique calling and purpose in life and provides the practical guidelines that enable you to remain faithful to that call. "

David Wraight
President, Youth for Christ International

"Sean Dunn has surrendered his life and lives to contend for this generation. *The Warrior Way* is another example of God using him to make an incredible difference. I know of no greater need for this generation of young men than to hear and understand God's call to be a warrior. Thanks to Sean, we now have a clear understanding of the call and are given a pathway to live the life of a warrior."

Dr. Chuck Stecker
President, Founder
A Chosen Generation, Inc.

"Sean offers great insight and practical wisdom while remaining personable. *The Warrior Way* will both encourage and challenge you as you seek to discover the treasures that God placed inside of you. You will gain understanding and discover courage as you seek to progress in your personal journey of faith. This is a great read."

Sarah Bowling-co host with her mother
Marilyn Hicky on "Today with Marilyn and Sarah."

"When Christ died on the cross and rose from the dead, He launched a revolution. Today, He is enlisting warriors that will advance His Kingdom on the planet. *The Warrior Way* will give you confidence to surrender your life and join the revolution. Excellent Book!"

David Perkins
Director of Desperation

"In *The Warrior Way*, Sean empowers people with an awareness that something must be done in the earth today to advance the Kingdom of God. He shows ordinary and imperfect people can get it done. While revisiting the lives of everyday heroes in the Bible, Sean openly shares the struggles and successes of his own journey which ignites a sense of confidence that God can and will use anyone willing to enter the battle."

Nate Rees, Singer, Songwriter, and
Worship Leader for Nameless Worship